LITERATURE FOR ENGLISH

INTERMEDIATE ONE

Burton Goodman

McGraw-Hill
Contemporary

Project Manager: Christine Lund Orciuch
Series Editor: Anne Petti Smith
Executive Editor: Linda Kwil
Creative Director: Michael E. Kelly
Marketing Manager: Sean Klunder
Production Manager: Genevieve Kelley

McGraw-Hill
Contemporary

Send all inquiries to:

McGraw-Hill/Contemporary
One Prudential Plaza
130 E. Randolph Ave. Suite 400
Chicago, IL 60601

ISBN: 0-07-256515-2

Printed in the United States of America.

1 2 3 4 5 6 7 8 9 10 QPD 07 06 05 04 03 02

The McGraw·Hill Companies

CONTENTS

Acknowledgments

Acknowledgment is gratefully made to the following publishers, authors, and agents for permission to reprint these works. Adaptations and/or abridgments are by Burton Goodman. Retellings of "Dr. Heidegger's Experiment" by Nathaniel Hawthorne and "Fire" from "To Build a Fire" by Jack London are by Burton Goodman. All rights reserved.

"Something Funny" by Elizabeth Van Steenwyk. Reprinted by permission of Elizabeth Van Steenwyk.

"Three Hundred Pesos" by Manuela Williams Crosno. Copyright © 1987 by Manuela Williams Crosno. Adapted and reprinted by permission of the author's agent, Burton Goodman.

"Younde Goes to Town" from *The Cow-Tail Switch and Other West African Stories* by Harold Courlander and George Herzog. Copyright © 1947, 1975 by Harold Courlander.

"Six Rows of Flowers" by Toshio Mori. From *Yokohama, California* by Toshio Mori. Copyright © 1985 by Toshio Mori. Reprinted by permission of the Caxton Press, Caldwell, Idaho.

"Space Star" by Lael J. Littke. "Space Princess" originally published in *The Friend* Magazine, March 1979. Copyright © 1979. Reprinted by permission of the Sternig & Byrne Literary Agency.

"The Contest" by William Hoffman. Copyright © 1964 by Scholastic Magazines.

TO THE TEACHER

Literature for English is a literature-based skills program designed to help readers improve their basic English skills.

Each book in the series contains outstanding stories by famous writers. The language in the stories is controlled so that they can be easily understood by students. Depending on the level, the stories are divided into a number of short, illustrated sections to assist the reader in understanding the selection. Many of the chapters in the Advanced Levels contain theme-related stories and poems.

A pre-reading section entitled **GETTING READY TO READ** introduces each story in this book. The component parts, **The Story and You, Learning About Literature,** and **Looking Ahead,** provide high-interest material to motivate the learner to read the story that follows. This section also offers important information about elements of literature.

Each story is followed by a comprehensive four-part skills check that is specially developed to meet the needs of LEP readers and is consistent with the general scope and sequence for ESL curricula.

The skills check provides a wide variety of hands-on practice in reading, writing, speaking, and listening. It includes the following exercises:

CHECK YOUR READING Ten self-scoring multiple-choice questions review reading comprehension, vocabulary, and idioms in the story just read. A Score Chart at the end of the book enables readers to enter their scores and see their results.

UNDERSTANDING THE STORY Varied exercises use directed writing activities for mastery of reading comprehension, sentence structure, verbs, parts of speech, writing, and punctuation. Hints to help the reader improve spelling and grammar are offered throughout.

STUDYING THE STORY Post-reading activities provide opportunities for students to work together to improve their listening, speaking, and writing skills. Specific as well as open-ended writing assignments and exercises appear in the sections **Studying the Story** and in the final section, **THINKING ABOUT LITERATURE**. Readers also complete a graphic organizer for each selection.

Literary elements explored in this series include character, plot, setting, conflict, and theme, as well as genre, such as the folktale, science fiction, and autobiography. In addition, this book contains features designed to teach and reinforce critical reading skills, such as making predictions, drawing conclusions, and reaching a decision by making inferences.

The vocabulary for each book in the series is drawn primarily from core word lists for beginning, intermediate, and advanced level students. Skills development is progressive, although it is possible to alter the sequence for intermediate and advanced level readers.

It should be noted that the Beginning book and Intermediate books use line reference numbers in the margins of the stories. These are extremely useful not only in helping the reader locate specific answers, but also in providing easy reference for reinforcement and review. The Beginning and Intermediate books also contain certain words and phrases printed in **boldfaced** type. This identifies the vocabulary and idioms that readers are tested on in the multiple-choice section following each chapter.

The Teacher's Guide provides the Answer Key for scoring **CHECK YOUR READING**, as well as suggested answers for the exercises in **UNDERSTANDING THE STORY**. At the back of the book is a list of Irregular Verbs, including their present and past tenses and their past participles.

I appreciate the contributions of the many teachers, students, administrators, and ESL coordinators who offered assistance in the development of the *Literature for English* series. For their valuable suggestions, I am grateful.

The program's fine literature, attractive format, and positive approach should encourage the reader to enjoy literature and to improve their English.

Burton Goodman

SCOPE & SEQUENCE

Story	Reading Skills	Literary Elements	Grammar Structures
Something Funny *page 1*	■ drawing conclusions	■ surprise endings	■ past tense (regular verbs) ■ verb *to be* (past tense)
Three Hundred Pesos *page 23*	■ making predictions ■ comparison & contrast	■ characterization	■ past tense (irregular verbs) ■ pronouns ■ verb *to have* (present tense)
Younde Goes To Town *page 53*		■ *style:* folktale	■ changing positive sentences to negative (*didn't*) ■ punctuation ■ past perfect tense ■ prepositions
Fire *page 75*	■ making inferences	■ setting ■ main character	■ adjectives ■ adverbs
Dr. Heidegger's Experiment *page 97*	■ finding the main idea	■ theme ■ symbol	■ changing statements to questions ■ comparing adjectives and adverbs ■ past continuous tense
Six Rows of Flowers *page 121*		■ *style:* autobiography ■ narrator	■ future tense (*will* + verb) ■ possessive pronouns ■ past tense (irregular verbs) ■ punctuation
Space Star *page 145*	■ summarizing	■ *style:* science fiction	■ present perfect tense ■ combining sentences ■ verbs *to go* and *to fly* ■ changing statements to questions
The Contest *page 167*	■ comparison & contrast	■ conflict ■ motive	■ past perfect tense ■ distinguishing between present, past, and future tenses ■ distinguishing between present perfect, past perfect, & past continuous tenses

SOMETHING FUNNY

BY ELIZABETH VAN STEENWYK

GETTING READY TO READ

1. The Story and You

In "Something Funny," you will meet Janey and Bill. Bill tells Janey a dream that is about a large flying saucer with flashing lights. Do you believe in flying saucers? Tell why.

2. Learning About Literature

"Something Funny" has a **surprise ending**. A surprise ending means that the ending is different from what most readers expect. Sometimes, the author gives *clues* to help the reader figure out and understand the surprise. See if the ending to this story surprises *you*.

3. Looking Ahead

This story is called "Something Funny." The word *funny* can have two meanings. It can mean "amusing" or "odd or strange." Look at the picture on the left. Which meaning of the word *funny* do you think is the right one for this story? What kind of day do you think it is? What kind of feeling do you get on days like this? Where do you think the story takes place? Read on to see if you are right.

SOMETHING FUNNY

BY ELIZABETH VAN STEENWYK

PART 1

Janey nervously **paced** up and down the floor of her living room. Bill was late for their date again. She liked Bill when she met him two months ago. But now she was getting tired of him. It wasn't because he was late all the time. The problem was that he wasn't too interesting. To tell the truth, he was very boring.

"Maybe I should tell him tonight that I don't want to go out with him anymore," Janey thought to herself. Then she heard a car screeching as it stopped outside. She looked out the window. It was raining so hard it was difficult to see, but she was able to recognize Bill's car at the curb.[1]

Janey quickly put on her coat. Then she hurried outside, slamming the door behind her.

By the time she got to the car, her coat was **drenched** from the rain. "I wonder how long this storm will last," Janey said to herself, as Bill came up to meet her.

Bill opened the car door. "I'm sorry I'm late," he apologized, "but I really couldn't help it."

"We better hurry," said Janey as she got into the car.

"First let me tell you what happened," said Bill, as he sat down beside her.

"You can tell me on the way," Janey said impatiently.[2]

Bill stepped on the gas pedal and headed for the country. Someone Bill knew was having a party at an old, **abandoned** farmhouse about twenty miles away. It was a little unusual, but it was certainly better than staying at home watching *Star Wars* again. Bill loved that movie. He had seen it **at least** a dozen times.

---

1. *curb:* the raised edge along a sidewalk

2. *impatiently:* in a hurry

"I don't know how to begin," Bill said. "The whole thing was so strange."

"What was strange?" Janey asked. "The reason you were late?"

30 "Yes," said Bill. "You see, I got home early from work, so I decided to lie down and read the newspaper."

"And you fell asleep?" Janey said.

"How did you know that?" Bill asked, looking surprised.

"That's not the first time you've done that," said Janey. "What 35 happened then?"

"I had the weirdest[3] dream," said Bill. "I dreamed that there was a terrible storm. It was actually a tornado[4]. . . ."

"A tornado?" said Janey. "We had a tornado warning a few hours ago. I heard it on the radio."

40 "Really?" said Bill. "That's weird, too. Anyway, a flying saucer[5] suddenly flew out of the tornado. It was large and had flashing lights. The flying saucer stopped outside my window and some people got out."

Janey shivered slightly as she looked out the window at the dark, shadowy countryside. "What did the people look like?" she asked.

45 "They didn't look like anyone I've ever seen before," said Bill. He paused, then he added, "They had . . ."

Bill took his eyes off the road and looked at Janey. "They had . . ."

"Bill!" shouted Janey. "Keep your eyes on the road!"

Janey tried to look outside, but it was raining so hard she had trouble 50 seeing beyond the windshield.[6] "Bill," she said, "maybe you should wait until we get to the party before you tell me the rest of your dream."

---

3. *weird:* strange, not usual

4. *tornado:* a kind of storm that has very strong, twisting winds

5. *a flying saucer:* a round spaceship. A spaceship comes from another planet.

6. *windshield:* the sheet of glass at the front of a car. The driver looks through the windshield.

CHECK YOUR READING

Put an **X** in the box next to the correct answer.

How many questions did you answer correctly? Circle your score. Then fill in your score on the Score Chart on page 190.

Number Correct	Score
1	10
2	20
3	30
4	40
5	50
6	60
7	70
8	80
9	90
10	100

Reading Comprehension

1. When did Janey meet Bill?
   - ☐ **a.** a week ago
   - ☐ **b.** a month ago
   - ☐ **c.** two months ago

2. Janey thought that Bill was
   - ☐ **a.** very interesting.
   - ☐ **b.** not too interesting.
   - ☐ **c.** going to be early for their date.

3. Bill and Janey were going to a farmhouse that was about
   - ☐ **a.** a mile away.
   - ☐ **b.** ten miles away.
   - ☐ **c.** twenty miles away.

4. Bill loved to
   - ☐ **a.** play football.
   - ☐ **b.** watch *Star Wars.*
   - ☐ **c.** listen to the radio.

5. After Bill came home, he
   - ☐ **a.** fell asleep while he was reading the newspaper.
   - ☐ **b.** went to see a movie.
   - ☐ **c.** made a telephone call.

6. Bill dreamed that a flying saucer
   - ☐ **a.** crashed into his house.
   - ☐ **b.** landed on top of his car.
   - ☐ **c.** stopped outside his window.

Vocabulary

7. Janey paced up and down the floor of her living room. The word *paced* means
   - ☐ **a.** fixed.
   - ☐ **b.** walked.
   - ☐ **c.** cleaned.

8. Her coat was drenched by the rain. The word *drenched* means
   - ☐ **a.** made very bright.
   - ☐ **b.** made very short.
   - ☐ **c.** made very wet.

9. The party was at an old, abandoned farmhouse. The word *abandoned* means
   - ☐ **a.** empty.
   - ☐ **b.** little.
   - ☐ **c.** beautiful.

Idioms

10. Bill had seen *Star Wars* at least a dozen times. The idiom *at least* means
    - ☐ **a.** less than.
    - ☐ **b.** more than.
    - ☐ **c.** worse than.

UNDERSTANDING THE STORY

Exercise A ~ **Checking Comprehension**

Answer each question by writing a complete sentence. Begin each sentence with a capital letter, and end each sentence with a period. You may use the line numbers in parentheses to help you. The first sentence has been done for you.

1. When did Janey meet Bill? (3)

   She met him two months ago.

2. Why was Janey getting tired of Bill? (5)

   _____

3. What did Janey hear outside? (7)

   _____

4. How far away was the old farmhouse? (24)

   _____

5. How many times had Bill seen *Star Wars*? (26)

   _____

6. What did Bill do when he got home early from work? (31)

   _____

7. What flew out of the tornado? (40)

   _____

8. What did the flying saucer look like? (41)

   _____

9. Where did the flying saucer stop? (42)

   _____

10. Why did Janey have trouble seeing beyond the windshield? (49)

    _____

Exercise B ~ Building Sentences

Make sentences by adding the correct letter. The first sentence has been done for you.

1. __*e*__ Bill was late   **a.** saw Bill's car.

2. _____ When Janey looked outside, she   **b.** would last.

3. _____ Janey left the house, slamming   **c.** at a farmhouse.

4. _____ She wondered how long the storm   **d.** the door behind her.

5. _____ They were going to a party   **e.** all the time.

Now do questions 6–10 the same way.

6. _____ Bill fell asleep while he was   **a.** Bill had ever seen before.

7. _____ The flying saucer was large and   **b.** look at the road.

8. _____ The people didn't look like anyone   **c.** reading the newspaper.

9. _____ Janey looked out the window at   **d.** had flashing lights.

10. _____ Janey wanted Bill to   **e.** the dark countryside.

Now write the sentences on the lines below. Remember to begin each sentence with a capital letter and to end each sentence with a period.

1. _____

2. _____

3. _____

4. _____

5. _____

6. _____

7. _____

8. _____

9. _____

10. _____

Exercise C ~ Adding Vocabulary

In the box are 8 words from the story. Complete each sentence by adding the correct word. The first one has been done for you.

recognize	impatiently	tornado	weird
boring	shivered	screeching	apologized

1. Bill wasn't very interesting. He was _____*boring*_____ .

2. Janey heard a high, loud noise. It was a car, which was

   _____ to a stop.

3. It was hard for Janey to see. However, she was able to

   _____ Bill's car.

4. Bill was sorry that he was late. He _____ to Janey.

5. Janey knew that they were late. "We better hurry," she said

   _____.

6. Bill had a very strange dream. Everything that happened in it was

   _____.

7. A terrible storm was on the way. It was a _____.

8. Janey felt frightened. She _____ as she looked out
   the window.

Exercise D ~ Using Verbs Correctly

Fill in each blank using the **past tense** of one of the regular verbs in the box. The first one has been done for you.

ask	hurry	like	dry	try
stop	watch	worry	look	open

Remember, when you write the **past tense** of most verbs that end in *y,* you must change the *y* to an *i* and add *ed.*

Example: cry becomes cr*ied.*

1. At first, Janey _____*liked*_____ Bill.

2. Bill's car slowed down and _____ at the curb.

3. Janey _____ out the window at the countryside.

4. Janey put on her coat and quickly _____ outside.

5. Bill _____ the car door and Janey got into the car.

6. Janey's wet hair _____ very quickly.

7. They often _____ *Star Wars* together.

8. Janey _____ Bill, "What was so strange?"

9. Janey was _____ about the way Bill was driving.

10. She _____ to make Bill drive carefully.

Exercise E ~ Putting Words in Order

Unscramble each sentence by putting the words in the correct order. Add *s* to the verb when necessary. Write each sentence on the line. The first one has been done for you. Each sentence is in the **present tense.**

1. about / This / Janey and Bill / tell / story.

   This story tells about Janey and Bill.

2. think / that / She / very interesting / is not /Bill

   _____

3. again and again /*Star Wars* / enjoy / Bill / seeing

   _____

4. her house / hear / outside / Bill's car /Janey

   _____

5. in / get / car / Bill's / They

   _____

6. hard / It / rain / begin / very / to

   _____

7. twenty / Bill and Janey / miles / drive

   _____

Before You Read Part 2

In Part 1, Bill told Janey the beginning of his "weird dream." He said that the people in the flying saucer didn't look like anyone he had ever seen before. Bill seemed very surprised. What do you think the space people looked like? See if you are right.

PART 2

Bill sighed, looked closely at the road, and concentrated[1] on driving. Janey stared out the window again. It was not raining as hard as before, but the wind had **increased**. She saw branches flying across the road. Now and then a few branches were hurled
5 against the car. She could hear them hitting the roof and the windshield. Bill began to drive more slowly. Then he turned onto a country lane.

"Are you sure this is the right road?" asked Janey. "It's so dark out here. How do you know where to drive?"

10 "I know," said Bill. "I was at a party here last year."

"You were?" Janey asked. That didn't sound like Bill at all. He wasn't the kind of person who went to parties in deserted places. He was so dull.[2] He was only interested in flying saucers and spaceships and that sort of thing. Was he more interesting than she realized?
15 Was he smarter than she thought? Janey wondered about that.

"Tell me more about your dream, Bill," Janey said.

"Oh, sure," he said. "I never had a dream that seemed so real. It was as if I were *really* living it, if you know what I mean. Anyway, some funny-looking people **exited** from the flying saucer and told
20 me to follow them. I did what they said."

"Where did you go?" Janey asked. She wished that they would drive by another house so she could see lights and people again.

"I went inside the flying saucer," Bill said. "And when I got inside, there was another *me* there. He was a replacement, they said. A
25 replacement for me."

"A replacement?" said Janey.

"Yes. You know, someone who looks and talks exactly like I do."

Janey held back a laugh. "Are you telling me that I'm going out with a replacement tonight?" she asked.

30 "How would I know?" asked Bill. "Would I really know if I'm a replacement?"

---

1. *concentrated:* thought about carefully

2. *dull:* boring, not interesting

Janey said, "You probably wouldn't know if you were a robot.[3] But if you weren't a robot, you'd know that you were someone from space—that you were a replacement who was here in disguise."

35 "Hey, Janey, that's good," Bill said. "I didn't realize that you knew so much about this space stuff."

"How many times have we watched *Star Wars* together?" she asked.

Bill grinned as Janey said, "But I have a question for you. Why 40 would *you* be replaced—why *you* of all people?"

Bill thought for a moment and answered, "Maybe it's because I'm so interested in space. You know, maybe I could communicate[4] with them or something like that."

"Maybe," Janey said softly to herself. "Or maybe," she thought, 45 "it's because you're not very interesting. No one really **pays attention** to you. If space people filled the earth with people like you, the earth would never know it until it was too late."

"Hey," said Bill, as he turned the car sharply to **avoid** a branch in the road, "maybe *all* of us are going to be replaced tonight."

50 "Stop it right now!" Janey said. "I've heard enough of that kind of talk!"

A few minutes later there were lights in the clearing ahead. Then they saw the outline of an old farmhouse against the dark sky.

Bill said, "I forgot to tell you something about the people in the 55 flying saucer. They each had three eyes. They had two eyes where we have ours. Then they had an extra eye in the middle of their foreheads."[5] Bill started to laugh. "That was funny, I tell you."

Janey looked at Bill. He was still laughing loudly as he drove along. Bill had the strangest sense of humor. They had three eyes. 60 What was so funny about that?

3. *robot:* a machine that can do some of the things that people can do

4. *communicate:* to speak or write to someone else or others

5. *forehead:* the part of the face above the eyes

Bill parked in a place between two other cars. They heard music and laughter coming from the house. Bill turned off the engine.

"Well," he said, "let's go inside and see if our replacements are here." Then he tried to laugh like one of those monsters on TV.

65 He got out of the car and walked around to Janey's side. Suddenly, Janey couldn't stand it any longer. She was tired of Bill. She was tired of being with him, tired of **pretending** to be somebody else. She wanted to be with someone more like herself, someone she could really talk to. She knew what she had to do.

70 As Bill opened the car door, Janey said softly to him, "Hey, Bill. Do you want to see something funny?" She reached up to her forehead, pushed away her hair, and quickly pulled off a flat bandage.

Bill stared in shock at Janey's forehead. He stared at the third eye
75 there.

Read the last paragraph of the story again. What can you figure out, or *conclude*, about Janey? What information in the story helps you arrive at this conclusion? Often, clues and facts help the reader make, or draw, a conclusion. When you **draw a conclusion**, you use information in the story to reach a decision.

Meet the Author

Elizabeth Van Steenwyk was born in 1928. She grew up in Illinois. She has written many books and more than 200 short stories. Some of her books have been made into movies and TV programs. One of her books, *The Best Horse,* became an award-winning film. Van Steenwyk now lives in California. She loves to write, and she also teaches writing. She tells her students "If you want to be a writer, you must write, write, write. Work as hard as you can and never give up."

CHECK YOUR READING

Put an **X** in the box next to the correct answer.

Reading Comprehension

1. Bill knew the way to the farmhouse because he
   - ☐ **a.** lived near it.
   - ☐ **b.** visited it often.
   - ☐ **c.** went to a party there last year.

2. Janey said that Bill was only interested in
   - ☐ **a.** reading the newspaper.
   - ☐ **b.** flying saucers and spaceships.
   - ☐ **c.** baseball and basketball.

3. Bill thought that his dream was very
   - ☐ **a.** sad.
   - ☐ **b.** funny.
   - ☐ **c.** real.

4. What did Bill see inside the flying saucer?
   - ☐ **a.** someone who looked and talked like him
   - ☐ **b.** some other people from Earth
   - ☐ **c.** several robots

5. The people in the flying saucer had
   - ☐ **a.** green skin.
   - ☐ **b.** blue hair.
   - ☐ **c.** three eyes.

Vocabulary

6. As the wind increased, branches flew across the road. The word *increased* means
   - ☐ **a.** got stronger.
   - ☐ **b.** got weaker.
   - ☐ **c.** stopped.

7. Some funny-looking people exited from the flying saucer. The word *exited* means
   - ☐ **a.** went into.
   - ☐ **b.** went out of.
   - ☐ **c.** thought about.

8. Bill tried to avoid a branch in the road. The word *avoid* means
   - ☐ **a.** to hit.
   - ☐ **b.** to throw.
   - ☐ **c.** to keep away from.

9. Janey was tired of pretending to be someone else. The word *pretending* means
   - ☐ **a.** acting like.
   - ☐ **b.** asking questions.
   - ☐ **c.** enjoying very much.

Idioms

10. She said, "No one really pays attention to Bill." The idiom to *pay attention to* means
    - ☐ **a.** to give money.
    - ☐ **b.** to give help.
    - ☐ **c.** to listen to, or notice.

How many questions did you answer correctly? Circle your score. Then fill in your score on the Score Chart on page 190.

Number Correct	Score
1	10
2	20
3	30
4	40
5	50
6	60
7	70
8	80
9	90
10	100

Understanding the Story

Exercise A ~ **Checking Comprehension**

Answer each question by writing a complete sentence. Begin each sentence with a capital letter, and end each sentence with a period. You may use the line numbers in parentheses to help you.

1. What hit the roof and the windshield of the car? (4)

2. What was Bill interested in? (13)

3. Who exited from the flying saucer? (19)

4. What did Bill see inside the flying saucer? (24)

5. Why did Bill turn the car sharply? (48)

6. What was unusual about the people in the flying saucer? (55)

7. Where did Bill park? (61)

8. What did Bill and Janey hear coming from the house? (61)

9. What did Janey pull off her forehead? (72)

10. At the end of the story, what did Bill stare at? (74)

Exercise B ~ Building Sentences

Make sentences by adding the correct letter.

1. _____ There were branches flying
2. _____ Janey wondered if Bill
3. _____ Bill went inside
4. _____ A robot can do

5. _____ They had seen *Star Wars*

a. the flying saucer.

b. across the road.

c. many times before.

d. was smarter than she realized.

e. some things that people can do.

Now do questions 6–10 the same way.

6. _____ Bill said that he was

7. _____ After driving a long way, they

8. _____ They heard music coming

9. _____ Janey wanted to be with someone who

10. _____ She reached up and pushed

a. saw lights in the clearing.

b. away her hair.

c. was more like herself.

d. interested in space.

e. from the house.

Now write the sentences on the lines below. Remember to begin each sentence with a capital letter and to end each sentence with a period.

1. _____

2. _____

3. _____

4. _____

5. _____

6. _____

7. _____

8. _____

9. _____

10. _____

Exercise C ~ Adding Vocabulary

In the box are 8 words from the story. Complete each sentence by adding the correct word.

lane	concentrated	monsters	disguise
communicate	dull	deserted	outline

1. Bill looked closely at the road and ＿＿＿＿＿＿＿＿＿ on driving.

2. After a while, Bill drove onto a dark country ＿＿＿＿＿＿＿＿＿.

3. The farmhouse was in a lonely, ＿＿＿＿＿＿＿＿＿ place somewhere in the country.

4. Bill was not very interesting; Janey thought that he was

＿＿＿＿＿＿＿＿＿.

5. Could he be someone from space who was here on Earth in

＿＿＿＿＿＿＿＿＿?

6. Bill began to laugh like one of the ＿＿＿＿＿＿＿＿＿ on TV.

7. They saw the ＿＿＿＿＿＿＿＿＿ of the farmhouse against the sky.

8. Bill wondered if he could ＿＿＿＿＿＿＿＿＿ with someone from space.

Exercise D ~ Using Verbs Correctly

Fill in each blank using the past tense of the verb *to be (was, were)*.

Remember that the past tense of the verb *to be* does not follow the usual rules. The correct way to write this verb is shown on the chart below.

Singular (one)		Plural (more than one)	
I	was	we	were
you	were	you	were
he/she/it	was	they	were

1. It _____ hard for Janey to see.

2. Branches _____ flying across the road.

3. Bill said, "I _____ at a party here last year."

4. Bill's dream _____ very real.

5. There _____ some funny-looking people in the flying saucer.

6. Bill _____ interested in space and flying saucers.

7. There _____ lights in the clearing ahead.

8. Music and laughter _____ coming from the house.

9. Janey _____ tired of Bill.

10. At the end of the story, Bill _____ shocked.

Begin each sentence by writing **Was** or **Were**.

11. _____ Bill driving very slowly?

12. _____ Janey and Bill going to a party?

13. _____ the people in the flying saucer friendly to Bill?

14. _____ Janey a visitor from space?

15. _____ the ending of the story a surprise to you?

Exercise E ~ True or False?

Write **T** if the sentence is true. Write **F** if the sentence is false.

1. _____ Bill was driving to a party on a sunny day.

2. _____ Bill was not interested in flying saucers.

3. _____ Janey could hear branches hitting the roof of the car.

4. _____ Janey wondered if Bill was more interesting than she realized.

5. _____ Bill told Janey about a dream that seemed very real.

6. _____ Janey and Bill had never seen *Star Wars* together.

7. _____ A robot can do some things that people can do.

8. _____ The people in the flying saucer had five eyes.

9. _____ Janey never got tired of talking to Bill.

10. _____ At the end of the story, Bill stared at Janey's forehead.

Exercise F ~ Vocabulary Review

Write a complete sentence for each word.

1. boring _____

_____

2. shivered _____

_____

3. recognize _____

_____

4. impatiently _____

_____

5. paced _____

_____

6. monsters _____

_____

7. lane _____

_____

8. communicate _____

_____

9. concentrated _____

_____

10. increased _____

_____

STUDYING THE STORY

A. Looking Back at the Story

Discuss these questions with your partner or with the group. Your teacher may ask you to write your answer to one of the questions.

- Why is the story called "Something Funny"?

- Bill thought that people with three eyes looked very funny. Janey didn't think so. Explain why.

- Why did Janey pull the bandage off at the end of the story?

B. Charting the Story

Look back at the story to get the information you need to complete the plot in the story map below. The **plot** tells the important events that take place, or happen, in the story. The first two events in the plot are listed. Compare your story map with those of your neighbors. Share your ideas about the story map.

Title: Something Funny

Characters: Janey and Bill

Plot (the important events that take place in the story):

1. Janey was waiting for Bill to arrive.

2. Janey got into the car.

3. _____

4. _____

5. _____

6. _____

7. _____

THINKING ABOUT LITERATURE

1. What is the *surprise ending* to the story?

_____

_____

_____

_____

2. Now you can write your *own* surprise ending to the story. Pretend that the story ends with line 68. Suppose that Bill and Janey enter the farmhouse. What happens then? Here are some possible new endings:

- Everyone shouts "Surprise" at Janey. It is her birthday.
- Everyone in the house looks exactly like Bill.
- Everyone in the house looks exactly like Janey.
- Everyone in the house has three eyes and acts strangely.

Think of a surprise ending of your own—or use one or more of the above. Then write the new ending by adding 6–8 sentences.

Bill and Janey got out of the car. Then they walked up to the farmhouse and knocked on the door.

_____

_____

_____

_____

_____

_____

_____

_____

_____

Three Hundred Pesos

by Manuela Williams Crosno

Getting Ready to Read

1. The Story and You

In "Three Hundred Pesos," your will meet Emilio and Anastacio. Emilio and Anastacio are brothers, but they are very different from each other. In what ways are *you* like people in your family? How are you different?

2. Learning About Literature

There are many ways that a writer can tell about the **characters** in a story. The writer can describe what the characters look like. The writer can tell what the characters think about and say. The writer can also tell how the characters act. As you read "Three Hundred Pesos," you will learn a lot about the characters in the story. Look for all the ways that the writer tells about the characters in the story.

3. Looking Ahead

Most of the people in Manuela Williams Crosno's stories are Spanish settlers who lived on the land in what is today the state of New Mexico. Think about the title of the story. Look at the picture on the left. What can you tell about the characters in "Three Hundred Pesos"? When do you think the story takes place? Read on to see if you are right.

THREE HUNDRED PESOS

BY MANUELA WILLIAMS CROSNO

PART 1

Emilio Perea was visiting his sister, Berta. Emilio said, "Just to save one peso, our brother, Anastacio, would let me starve."

"How do you know that, Emilio?" Berta asked.

"I know it because of what happened yesterday," he answered.

5 Emilio shook his head sadly and said, "When we were children, Anastacio was different."

Berta sighed. "I remember those happy days very well. That was a long time ago. But tell me more about our brother. Why do you say he would let you starve?"

10 "Well, this is what happened," said Emilio. "I went to see Anastacio yesterday to ask him for a peso to buy medicine for my little boy, Pedro. Pedro has been sick for three days. He can't eat anything."

"Did he give you the peso?" asked Berta.

"No, he did not!" said Emilio. "He told me, 'You are **wasting**
15 **your breath**, Emilio. Pedro is not *my* child. *I'm* not married. I don't have *niños*[1] to worry about. Go away and don't bother me.' That is what he said to me, Berta."

"Our brother is no good," said Berta. She sighed again. "But don't worry. I'll give you a peso to get medicine for Pedro."

20 At that moment their brother, Anastacio Perea, was walking across his cornfield. It had been a good year with a lot of rain. Anastacio saw that his crop was good and green, and he was certain that he would be paid well when it ripened in the fall.

Soon he would have three hundred pesos. All his life, it seemed,

---

1. *niños:* the Spanish word for "small children"

he had worked hard for that exact amount. He would have it soon
because his crop was good, and he would sell it for a high price. High
in the warm, blue sky a crow flew over the field. It **sped** toward the
dark mountains to the west.

Anastacio shook his fist at the bird. "My corn is not for *you*!" he
shouted. "You are like my brother and my sister. You want to take
what is mine. I have nothing to give to any of you!"

Then, as he often did, he thought back to the day when his plan
was born.

He was a small boy and had asked the storekeeper, "How come
you never work?"

"*I* am the storekeeper," the man had replied, laughing.

For several days the young Anastacio thought about this amazing
piece of **information**. *His* father worked hard in the fields, as did
all of their neighbors.

Again he went to the storekeeper. "How much money does it take
to own a store?"

"Oh," said the storekeeper, "you need about three hundred pesos
to start." The storekeeper looked at the serious boy. "But that is a lot
of money," he warned.

From that day, Anastacio set a goal for himself. He *had* to earn
three hundred pesos! But that was not easy to do. Although he held
on to his money like a **miser**, he made some bad investments and
was unlucky in some other business matters. One time someone stole
money from his house. Since then he kept his pesos in a leather bag
under his shirt, tightly tied to his trouser belt.

Now Anastacio removed the leather bag from his belt and
counted his money. He had two hundred pesos. He would probably
get fifty pesos more from the sale of his corn. He looked out across
the field and was satisfied.

CHECK YOUR READING

Put an **X** in the box next to the correct answer.

How many questions did you answer correctly? Circle your score. Then fill in your score on the Score Chart on page 190.

Number Correct	Score
1	10
2	20
3	30
4	40
5	50
6	60
7	70
8	80
9	90
10	100

Reading Comprehension

1. Emilio Perea was visiting
- ☐ **a.** his brother, Anastacio.
- ☐ **b.** his sister, Berta.
- ☐ **c.** his son, Pedro.

2. Emilio asked Anastacio for
- ☐ **a.** one peso.
- ☐ **b.** ten pesos.
- ☐ **c.** one hundred pesos.

3. Pedro had been sick for
- ☐ **a.** a day.
- ☐ **b.** three days.
- ☐ **c.** a week.

4. Anastacio told Emilio
- ☐ **a.** to give him some money.
- ☐ **b.** to come back later.
- ☐ **c.** to go away.

5. Anastacio wanted to
- ☐ **a.** work for a storekeeper.
- ☐ **b.** live in a large house.
- ☐ **c.** save three hundred pesos.

6. Where did Anastacio keep his money?
- ☐ **a.** under his bed
- ☐ **b.** under his shirt
- ☐ **c.** in the bank

Vocabulary

7. The bird sped toward the mountains. The word *sped* means
- ☐ **a.** went quickly.
- ☐ **b.** fell slowly.
- ☐ **c.** looked carefully.

8. Young Anastacio thought about the amazing information the storekeeper gave him. The word *information* means
- ☐ **a.** candy.
- ☐ **b.** news.
- ☐ **c.** toys.

9. He held on to his money like a miser. A *miser* is a person who
- ☐ **a.** enjoys spending money.
- ☐ **b.** loves money and hates to spend it.
- ☐ **c.** gives money to friends.

Idioms

10. Anastacio told Emilio, "You are wasting your breath." When you are *wasting your breath,* you are
- ☐ **a.** running very fast.
- ☐ **b.** feeling tired.
- ☐ **c.** wasting your time.

UNDERSTANDING THE STORY

Exercise A ~ Checking Comprehension

Answer each question by writing a complete sentence. Begin each sentence with a capital letter, and end each sentence with a period. You may use the line numbers in parentheses to help you.

1. Who was Emilio Perea visiting? (1)

_____

2. Why did Emilio go to see Anastacio? (11)

_____

3. How long had Pedro been sick? (12)

_____

4. What did Berta say she would give Emilio? (19)

_____

5. How was Anastacio's crop? (22)

_____

6. Where did Anastacio's father work? (38)

_____

7. How much money did Anastacio want to earn? (46)

_____

8. Where did Anastacio keep his money now? (49)

_____

9. How much money did Anastacio have? (52)

_____

10. How much money did Anastacio expect to get from the sale of his corn? (53)

_____

Exercise B ~ Building Sentences

Make sentences by adding the correct letter.

1. _____ Emilio shook his head sadly   **a.** be paid well for the corn.

2. _____ Pedro did not eat because he   **b.** any children.

3. _____ Anastacio did not have   **c.** when he thought about Anastacio.

4. _____ Anastacio knew that he would   **d.** was sick.

5. _____ Anastacio thought that he would   **e.** sell his corn in the fall.

Now do questions 6–10 the same way.

6. _____ Anastacio's father worked   **a.** from Anastacio's house.

7. _____ Anastacio wanted to   **b.** the sale of his corn.

8. _____ The storekeeper looked   **c.** own a store.

9. _____ Someone once stole some money   **d.** in the fields.

10. _____ Anastacio thought that he could get fifty pesos from   **e.** at the serious young boy.

Now write the sentences on the lines below. Remember to begin each sentence with a capital letter and to end each sentence with a period.

1. _____

2. _____

3. _____

4. _____

5. _____

6. _____

7. _____

8. _____

9. _____

10. _____

Exercise C ~ Adding Vocabulary

In the box are 8 words from the story. Complete each sentence by adding the correct word.

leather	starve	investments	goal
crow	fist	medicine	ripened

1. Emilio needed to buy _____ for his son who was sick.

2. To save one peso, Anastacio was willing to let his brother

   _____ .

3. High in the sky, a _____ flew over the field.

4. Anastacio shouted at the bird and shook his _____ at it.

5. His _____ in life was to own a store.

6. He thought that he would be paid well when his corn

   _____ in the fall.

7. Anastacio lost money because he made some bad

   _____ .

8. He kept his money in a _____ bag under his shirt.

Exercise D ~ Using Verbs Correctly

Fill in each blank using the **past tense** of the irregular verb in parentheses. The first one has been done for you.

1. Emilio _____shook_____ his head sadly. (shake)

2. He _____, "When we were children, Anastacio was different." (say)

3. Emilio _____ to Anastacio to ask him for money. (go)

4. Anastacio _____ Emilio, "Don't bother me." (tell)

5. Anastacio _____ that his crop was good and green. (see)

6. The bird _____ across the sky and headed toward the mountain. (fly)

7. Anastacio _____ about when he was a little boy. (think)

8. Finally, he _____ three hundred pesos! (have)

9. He _____ on to his money and tried to spend as little as possible. (hold)

10. Anastacio _____ some mistakes and lost some pesos. (make)

11. Once, someone _____ some money from his house. (steal)

12. Now he _____ his money under his shirt. (keep)

Exercise E ~ Picking a Pronoun

Fill in the blank or blanks in each sentence by adding the correct pronoun.
Use each pronoun once.

I, me	**we, us**
you	**you**
he, she, it	**they**
him, her	**them**

Remember, a **pronoun** is a word that is used in place of a noun.

          noun   pronoun
Example: The *story* is short, but *it* is interesting.

1. Emilio needed some money, so _____ went to see Anastacio.

2. Anastacio did not want to talk to Emilio. Anastacio said to _____,

   "Don't bother _____."

3. When Emilio saw Berta, he told _____ about his visit to Anastacio.

4. Berta told Emilio, "_____ will give _____ a peso to buy
   medicine for Pedro."

5. Emilio said to Berta, "When _____ were children, Anastacio was

   different." "That was a long time ago, Emilio," _____ said.

6. Emilio and Berta felt sad when _____ thought about Anastacio.

7. Berta told Emilio, "Our brother doesn't care about you or me. He doesn't

   care about _____."

8. He kept his pesos hidden under his shirt. He didn't want anyone to steal

   _____.

9. His crop was very good. He could sell _____ for a lot of money.

10. Anastacio told his brother and sister, "I have nothing to give

    _____."

Before You Read Part 2

In Part 1, Emilio asked his brother Anastacio for one peso. However, Anastacio refused to give him a peso. Do you think Emilio or Berta will ask their brother for money again? See if you are right.

PART 2

That night there was a violent storm. Large pieces of hail fell over the village. The villagers declared that they had never seen hailstones as big as those. Windows were broken and trees were left bare. When the storm was over, all the corn in Anastacio's field was destroyed.

5 Anastacio stood beside his field and wondered what to do. His brother, Emilio, came along.

"Brother," said Emilio, "my corn is ruined too. It is a sad loss for us all. But corn is not everything in life. We can plant more corn. Come home with me and join us for a supper of tortillas and chile.
10 We can talk together then."

Anastacio was angry. He wanted to put the blame for the hail on his brother. He felt that in some strange way Emilio was responsible for this loss. He thought to himself, "If I had given Emilio money for his sick boy, would this have happened?" He wondered about it.

15 Anastacio became angrier. "Go home!" he shouted at his brother. "I have no time to eat with you!"

A few weeks later, Anastacio planted his corn again.

In July of that year, his sister, Berta, came to see him. She was thin and **frail** and seemed very uncomfortable. She sat down, pulling a
20 thin, black shawl over her face and shoulders. Her small face stared out from under the shawl and made her look like a frightened, starving bird.

Anastacio looked at her and wished that he had no relatives to bother him. It was obvious that his sister was in **distress**.

25 "Why have you come here?" he asked harshly. He had decided **to cut short** their talk.

"A tree fell on the roof of my *casa*."[1]

"So?" said Anastacio.

"We don't have the money to buy materials to make the repairs,"
30 Berta said. She paused, then went on. "If you can lend us a little money now, we will pay you back in a few weeks."

Anastacio thought about the money he had—of his pesos. He

_____

1. *casa:* the Spanish word for "house"

thought of the store he would own one day.

"I don't have any money to give you," he said quickly. Then he added, "And I don't have enough room here for you and your husband. Anyway, I only have enough food for myself."

Anastacio smiled and said, "Why don't you go to our brother, Emilio? Maybe *he* can give you some money. Maybe he can take you in."

Berta stood up and silently left the house. As she walked away, the wind blew against her shawl and lifted it up above her shoulders. Her shadow on the ground looked like a huge black bird. Anastacio suddenly had a feeling that something bad was going to happen. He tried not to think about it.

The next day Anastacio discovered that his field had been invaded by a flock of wandering sheep. The entire crop of corn was ruined. The **tender** young plants had been eaten or crushed, and it was too late now to plant again.

Later, Anastacio saw Berta on her way to the village. Emilio and his family were with her. Anastacio felt, somehow, that she was responsible for the ruined corn. Would things have been different if he had given her some money and allowed her to stay? He wondered about that. Anastacio looked bitterly in Berta's direction, but she did not see him. Her face was calm and peaceful.

CHECK YOUR READING

Put an **X** in the box next to the correct answer.

Reading Comprehension

1. The storm destroyed
   - ☐ **a.** Anastacio's house.
   - ☐ **b.** Anastacio's barn.
   - ☐ **c.** Anastacio's corn.

2. Emilio asked Anastacio to
   - ☐ **a.** join him for supper.
   - ☐ **b.** give him some money.
   - ☐ **c.** help him plant more corn.

3. When did Berta visit Anastacio?
   - ☐ **a.** in January
   - ☐ **b.** in June
   - ☐ **c.** in July

4. Berta said that a tree fell
   - ☐ **a.** into her garden.
   - ☐ **b.** on her fence.
   - ☐ **c.** on the roof of her house.

5. Berta asked if she could
   - ☐ **a.** borrow some money.
   - ☐ **b.** have some food.
   - ☐ **c.** live at Anastacio's house.

6. Anastacio discovered that his plants had been killed by
   - ☐ **a.** horses.
   - ☐ **b.** sheep.
   - ☐ **c.** wolves.

Vocabulary

7. Berta was thin and frail and looked like a starving bird. The word *frail* means
   - ☐ **a.** weak.
   - ☐ **b.** strong.
   - ☐ **c.** fat.

8. Berta was not comfortable; she was in distress. The word *distress* means
   - ☐ **a.** happiness or joy.
   - ☐ **b.** pain or sorrow.
   - ☐ **c.** beautiful clothing.

9. The animals crushed the tender young plants. The word *tender* means
   - ☐ **a.** soft.
   - ☐ **b.** hard.
   - ☐ **c.** old.

Idioms

10. Anastacio wanted his sister to leave, so he decided to cut short their talk. The idiom *to cut short* means
    - ☐ **a.** to attack.
    - ☐ **b.** to break.
    - ☐ **c.** to make shorter.

UNDERSTANDING THE STORY

Exercise A ~ Checking Comprehension

Answer each question by writing a complete sentence. Begin each sentence with a capital letter, and end each sentence with a period. You may use the line numbers in parentheses to help you.

1. What fell over the village during the storm? (1)

2. What did the storm do to the corn in Anastacio's field? (4)

3. Who did Anastacio think was responsible for the loss of his corn? (12)

4. What did Berta pull over her face and shoulders at Anastacio's house? (20)

5. What happened to the roof of Berta's house? (27)

6. Why did Berta need money? (29)

7. What did Berta's shadow look like? (41)

8. How did Anastacio feel when he saw Berta's shadow? (42)

9. What invaded Anastacio's field? (45)

10. What happened to the young plants in Anastacio's field? (46)

Exercise B ~ Building Sentences

Make sentences by adding the correct letter.

1. _____ The storm broke windows   **a.** planted his corn again.

2. _____ Emilio asked Anastacio   **b.** all over the village.

3. _____ A few weeks later, Anastacio   **c.** to join him for dinner.

4. _____ Berta said that she needed   **d.** in a few weeks.
          money to

5. _____ She said she would pay back   **e.** fix her roof.
          the money

Now do questions 6–10 the same way.

6. _____ Anastacio thought about   **a.** any money to give to
          the store   Berta.

7. _____ He said that he didn't have   **b.** left the house.

8. _____ Berta stood up and silently   **c.** she did not see him.

9. _____ Later, Anastacio saw Berta   **d.** he wanted to own.

10. _____ He looked in Berta's   **e.** on her way to the
          direction, but   village.

Now write the sentences on the lines below. Remember to begin each
sentence with a capital letter and to end each sentence with a period.

1. _____

2. _____

3. _____

4. _____

5. _____

6. _____

7. _____

8. _____

9. _____

10. _____

Exercise C ~ Adding Vocabulary

In the box are 8 words from the story. Complete each sentence by adding the correct word.

hailstones	violent	harshly	obvious
ruined	blame	shadow	materials

1. A _____ storm broke windows all over the village.

2. During the storm, large _____ fell everywhere.

3. The storm _____ Anastacio's corn.

4. Anastacio wanted to _____ Emilio and Berta for his losses.

5. As soon as Anastacio saw his unhappy sister, it was _____ to him that she needed help.

6. "Why have you come here?" the angry Anastacio asked

   _____ .

7. She needed money to buy _____ to fix the roof of her house.

8. When Anastacio saw his sister's _____ on the ground, he thought that something bad was going to happen.

Exercise D ~ Using Verbs Correctly

Fill in each blank using the **present tense** of the verb *to have (have, has)*.

Remember, the past tense of the verb *to have* does not follow the usual rules. The correct way to write this verb is shown on the chart below.

Singular		Plural	
(one)		(more than one)	
I	have	we	have
you	have	you	have
he/she/it	has	they	have

1. Anastacio _____ two hundred pesos.

2. Most of the villagers _____ a small piece of land.

3. Emilio _____ a son who is sick.

4. Berta and Emilio _____ many friends.

5. "I _____ no time to eat with you," Anastacio told his brother.

6. Her house _____ a hole in the roof.

7. "Why _____ you come here?" Anastacio asked Berta.

8. "We don't _____ enough money," Berta answered.

9. Emilio and Berta _____ supper together every Sunday.

10. She _____ a frightened look on her face.

11. "I only _____ enough food for myself," he said.

12. He _____ one brother and one sister.

Exercise E ~ Putting Events in Order

Part A

Put the events in the order in which they occurred. You may look back at the story. The first one has been done for you.

1. ___C___   **a.** Anastacio said that he did not have time to eat with Emilio.

2. _____   **b.** Emilio asked Anastacio to join him for supper.

3. _____   **c.** A storm destroyed the corn in Anastacio's field.

4. _____   **d.** Anastacio saw Berta as she was going to the village.

5. _____   **e.** Berta asked Anastacio to lend her some money.

6. _____   **f.** Anastacio wouldn't give Berta any money.

7. _____   **g.** Some sheep destroyed the corn in Anastacio's field.

Part B

Now list the correct order of the events on the lines below. The first one has been done for you.

1. *A storm destroyed the corn in Anastacio's field.*

2. _____

_____

3. _____

_____

4. _____

_____

5. _____

_____

6. _____

_____

7. _____

_____

Before You Read Part 3

In Part 1, Anastacio refused to give his brother one peso. In Part 2, Anastacio refused to lend his sister some money. Now Anastacio is ready to go to the village to sell his crop. Do you think that the story will have a happy ending or a sad ending? See if you are right.

PART 3

During the winter of that year, Anastacio earned fifty pesos by buying and then selling some horses. By spring he had two hundred and fifty pesos. He needed just fifty pesos more to have the amount he wanted. He did not see his brother or his sister anymore, but he heard from the neighbors that they were well and happy. "I hope they never bother me again!" he said to himself.

When spring came, the snow in the mountains melted and ran in streams down into the valleys. Then Anastacio planted his field. This time Anastacio planted pinto beans. He had heard they would sell for a high price because there had been a shortage of pinto beans the season before.

No one saw Anastacio all summer. He spent all of his time in the field. All day he worked in the field, and at night he slept there to guard it against sheep and other possible dangers.

In the fall Anastacio harvested his pinto beans. He put them in open wooden boxes and loaded them into his wagon. He had a large crop of fine beans ready to sell.

He left for the village. He hoped to sell the beans for fifty pesos. This would give him the amount he needed—three hundred pesos. At last! Yes, it would be his best winter. He could buy a store with the money. On cold winter days he would sit near the fire. He would have very little work to do and plenty to eat.

Although he had pleasant thoughts, Anastacio was not a happy man. Many things bothered him. He would have to guard his store very carefully. And he was worried about Berta and Emilio. They would think he was making a large profit. They would beg him for money. They would think that the food in his grocery store was free. They would think he should share it with them. Yes, all of these things worried Anastacio.

Anastacio drove along a narrow, winding road. It rose higher and higher before it **descended** into the valley where he planned to sell his beans. Anastacio finally reached the top of the road. His horses were **exhausted** from pulling the heavy load. But Anastacio was

impatient to get to the valley. He started down at once, urging on his
tired horses with a snap of the reins.

Anastacio turned around a curve as he went downhill. Suddenly
he was struck from behind by a fast-moving horseless wagon. The
driver did not see Anastacio in time to stop. He hit the back of
Anastacio's wagon, breaking off the piece of wood that held the
boxes of beans in place. This frightened the horses. They jumped up,
tipped the wagon, and threw Anastacio into the air. He fell
heavily against the trunk of a tree, hitting his head and his chest
with great force. The frightened horses ran wildly along the road and
scattered beans everywhere.

Anastacio was dazed, but he looked ahead and saw that the horses
had finally stopped by some trees near the home of his brother,
Emilio.

Anastacio turned around. He saw that, except for the broken
board, the wagon was not damaged. The horses did not seem to be
hurt either. This was good, but he had lost his crop again! All of his
boxes had been thrown out of the wagon. Beans were all over the
ground and in the ditch next to the road.

At this moment, the man in the horseless wagon returned. He
apologized for causing the accident. Then he saw all the beans along
the road and asked how much they were worth.

"Fifty pesos," gasped the unhappy Anastacio.

"**It's a deal**!" said the traveler, handing over the money. He was
glad to pay this amount and avoid further trouble.

Anastacio Perea was satisfied. When he was alone again, he took
the leather bag from his belt. He held the bag in one hand and the
fifty pesos in the other. There were two hundred and fifty pesos in
the bag, and now he had fifty pesos more. He could buy the store at
last. He was a rich man!

He sighed and sat down on the stump of a tree. His head ached
and his chest burned from the blow he had received. It was so hard

to breathe—

Suddenly he fell forward and lay very still in the warm sunshine. Three large, black birds circled slowly above him.

Anastacio's horses stopped a short distance from a field where Emilio and Berta were working. It was a warm morning, the crop was good, and they were very happy.

"Look!" shouted Emilio. "Those are our brother's horses!"

"But where is Anastacio?" asked Berta.

"Let's go and see!" said Emilio.

They hurried up the road together. Soon they came to the body of their brother. It was lying so still, they knew he was dead.

"Poor Anastacio!" exclaimed Emilio. "What terrible thing has happened to you?"

"Poor brother!" cried Berta. "I remember when you were a little boy. How we loved you then!"

Emilio took the money bag and the pesos from his brother's **clenched** hands. Emilio gave the money bag to Berta and looked at the pesos.

"There's so much money here," he said when he had finished counting. "Fifty pesos."

Berta opened the bag and took out the money.

"Two hundred and fifty pesos more!" she gasped in astonishment.

"Three hundred pesos!" they exclaimed together. "What a beautiful funeral he will have."

When you **make a prediction**, you guess about what is going to happen. Did you *guess* that the story was going to end happily or that it was going to end sadly? Did you *predict* correctly?

Meet the Author

Manuela Williams Crosno (1905–1977) lived most of her life in New Mexico. She loved the state, and she used it as the setting for her stories. They all take place in and around Santa Fe, Albuquerque, and Taos. Crosnos usually wrote about Spanish settlers who lived on the land more than one hundred years ago. Crosno taught English for many years. She was also a poet and an artist. Her article "Why I Teach School" won First Prize in a statewide writing contest.

CHECK YOUR READING

Put an **X** in the box next to the correct answer.

Reading Comprehension

1. By the spring Anastacio had
   - ☐ **a.** exactly fifty pesos.
   - ☐ **b.** nearly one hundred pesos.
   - ☐ **c.** two hundred and fifty pesos.

2. Anastacio planted pinto beans because he
   - ☐ **a.** loved to eat them.
   - ☐ **b.** planted them every year.
   - ☐ **c.** thought they would sell for a high price.

3. Anastacio's wagon was struck by
   - ☐ **a.** a horseless wagon.
   - ☐ **b.** a wild horse.
   - ☐ **c.** a large rock.

4. Anastacio fell against
   - ☐ **a.** the wagon.
   - ☐ **b.** the trunk of a tree.
   - ☐ **c.** a box of beans.

5. The traveler gave Anastacio
   - ☐ **a.** money.
   - ☐ **b.** bags filled with beans.
   - ☐ **c.** a new wagon.

6. Emilio and Berta knew that their brother was near when they saw
   - ☐ **a.** his horses.
   - ☐ **b.** his wagon.
   - ☐ **c.** the traveler.

Vocabulary

7. The road rose higher before it descended into the valley. The word *descended* means
   - ☐ **a.** went up.
   - ☐ **b.** went down.
   - ☐ **c.** went next to.

8. The horses were exhausted from pulling the heavy load. The word *exhausted* means very
   - ☐ **a.** tired.
   - ☐ **b.** happy.
   - ☐ **c.** smart.

9. Emilio took the bag and the pesos from his brother's clenched hands. The word *clenched* means
   - ☐ **a.** tired.
   - ☐ **b.** thin.
   - ☐ **c.** tightly closed.

Idioms

10. When Anastacio said the beans were worth fifty pesos, the traveler said, "It's a deal!" When you say *"It's a deal,"* you
    - ☐ **a.** are worried about something.
    - ☐ **b.** are happy about something.
    - ☐ **c.** agree to something.

How many questions did you answer correctly? Circle your score. Then fill in your score on the Score Chart on page 190.

Number Correct	Score
1	10
2	20
3	30
4	40
5	50
6	60
7	70
8	80
9	90
10	100

Understanding the Story

Exercise A ~ Checking Comprehension

Answer each question by writing a complete sentence. Begin each sentence with a capital letter, and end each sentence with a period. You may use the line numbers in parentheses to help you.

1. How much money did Anastacio earn by buying and selling horses? (1)

2. Why did Anastacio plant pinto beans? (9)

3. Why did Anastacio sleep in his field at night? (13)

4. How much money did Anastacio hope to get for his beans? (18)

5. What struck Anastacio's wagon from behind? (37)

6. What did Anastacio fall against? (42)

7. What did the traveler give Anastacio? (57)

8. Why did Anastacio think that he was a rich man? (62)

9. How did Berta and Emilio know that their brother was dead? (76)

10. What were Berta and Emilio going to do with Anastacio's money? (90)

Exercise B ~ Building Sentences

Build sentences by adding the correct letter.

1. _____ Anastacio did not see his brother   **a.** with the money he earned.

2. _____ He loaded the boxes of pinto beans   **b.** or his sister anymore.

3. _____ Anastacio wanted to buy a store   **c.** reached the top of the road.

4. _____ He was afraid that his brother and sister would   **d.** into his wagon.

5. _____ Anastacio finally   **e.** ask him for money.

Now do questions 6–10 the same way.

6. _____ A horseless wagon hit   **a.** circled above Anastacio.

7. _____ The frightened horses ran wildly   **b.** brother's body.

8. _____ Three large, black birds   **c.** took out the money.

9. _____ Berta and Emilio found their   **d.** along the road.

10. _____ Berta opened the bag and   **e.** Anastacio's wagon.

Now write the sentences on the lines below. Remember to begin each sentence with a capital letter and to end each sentence with a period.

1. _____

2. _____

3. _____

4. _____

5. _____

6. _____

7. _____

8. _____

9. _____

10. _____

Exercise C ~ Adding Vocabulary

In the box are 8 words from the story. Complete each sentence by adding the correct word.

dazed	ditch	winding	tipped
shortage	harvested	accident	scattered

1. Anastacio planted pinto beans because there had been a

    _____ of pinto beans last season.

2. When the beans were ready in the fall, Anastacio

    _____ them.

3. Anastacio drove along a narrow, _____ road that went higher and higher.

4. The other driver did not see Anastacio in time and caused the

    _____.

5. When the horses jumped up, they _____ the wagon and threw Anastacio into the air.

6. After Anastacio hit his head against the tree, he was

    _____.

7. The frightened horses ran wildly along the road and

    _____ the beans everywhere.

8. The beans were all over the ground and in the _____.

Exercise D ~ Using Verbs Correctly

Fill in each blank using the **past tense** of the irregular verb in parentheses.

1. Anastacio _____ from the neighbors that his brother and sister were well. (hear)

2. The snow in the mountains melted and _____ down into the valleys. (run)

3. Anastacio _____ all of his time in the field. (spend)

4. At night he _____ in the field to guard it against dangers. (sleep)

5. He _____ for the village early in the morning. (leave)

6. Anastacio _____ quickly because he was in a hurry. (drive)

7. A horseless wagon _____ the back of Anastacio's wagon. (strike)

8. The horses tipped the wagon and _____ Anastacio into the air. (throw)

9. Anastacio suddenly _____ forward. (fall)

10. Anastacio was very tired, so he _____ down. (sit)

11. He _____ very still in the warm sunshine. (lie)

12. Emilio and Berta _____ to the body of their brother. (come)

13. When they saw Anastacio on the ground, they _____ he was dead. (know)

14. Emilio _____ the money bag from his brother's hand. (take)

15. Then he _____ the money bag to Berta. (give)

Exercise E ~ Putting Events in Order

Part A

Put the events in the order in which they occurred. You may look back at the story.

1. _____   **a.** The traveler gave Anastacio fifty pesos.

2. _____   **b.** Anastacio hit his head against a tree.

3. _____   **c.** Berta and Emilio found Anastacio's body.

4. _____   **d.** Anastacio planted pinto beans.

5. _____   **e.** Anastacio's wagon was hit from behind by a fast-moving horseless wagon.

6. _____   **f.** Anastacio loaded his pinto beans into the wagon.

7. _____   **g.** Anastacio was thrown into the air.

Part B

Now list the correct order of events on the lines below.

1. _____

2. _____

3. _____

_____

4. _____

5. _____

6. _____

7. _____

Exercise F ~ Vocabulary Review

Write a complete sentence for each word.

1. medicine _____

_____

2. goal _____

_____

3. starve _____

_____

4. miser _____

_____

5. blame _____

_____

6. violent _____

_____

7. accident _____

_____

8. dazed _____

_____

9. shortage _____

_____

10. exhausted _____

_____

STUDYING THE STORY

A. Looking Back at the Story

Discuss these questions with your partner or with the group. Your teacher may ask you to write your answer to one of the questions.

- Why didn't Anastacio give his brother and sister some money?

- Suppose that Anastacio had given Berta money. Do you think his field would have been destroyed by sheep? Give reasons for your answer.

- Did you feel sorry for Anastacio at the end of the story—or did you think he deserved what happened to him? Explain your answer.

B. Charting Characters in a Story

A **Venn diagram** is a good way to show how characters in a story are different and alike. Look at the Venn diagram below. Notice that there are two circles that *overlap*, or cover each other, in the middle. In the circle marked **Anastacio**, write all the ways that Anastacio is different from Emilio. In the circle marked **Emilio**, write all the ways that Emilio is different from Anastacio. In the part that overlaps in the center, write how Anastacio and Emilio are alike. When you show how characters are different and alike, you **compare and contrast** them.

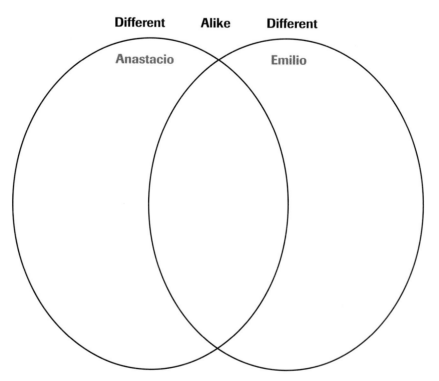

Different	Alike	Different
Anastacio		Emilio

THINKING ABOUT LITERATURE

1. Pick a character you have read about in another story or book. Remember to think about:

   ■ what the character looked like

   ■ how the character acted (what the character did)

   ■ things the character said

On the lines below, write about the character you chose. If you cannot think of a character from a story or book, write about a character from a movie or a TV show.

_____

Character's Name

_____

_____

_____

_____

_____

_____

2. Think of a different ending for "Three Hundred Pesos." Then write your ending on the lines below.

_____

_____

_____

_____

_____

_____

_____

_____

YOUNDE GOES TO TOWN

AN AFRICAN FOLKTALE

GETTING READY TO READ

1. The Story and You

In "Younde Goes to Town," a young man leaves his village for the first time. He travels to a town that is many miles away. Do you remember the first time that you went many miles from your home? Where did you go? Why did you go there? What questions did you ask the people who lived there?

2. Learning About Literature

"Younde Goes to Town" is an African **folktale**. The folktales we read today are stories that were first told, or "handed down," by many people over the years. Nearly every country has its own folktales. What is the name of a folktale you know? What happens in that folktale?

3. Looking Ahead

Look at the title and the picture on the left. In what land does the story take place? Do you think that the characters in the story live in a village or in a city? What kind of work do you think people there do? Read on to see if you are right.

Younde Goes to Town

An African Folktale

PART 1

Once in the country of Akim, in the hills far back from the coast, there was a man named Younde. He was a simple man who had never been far from home, and he spent his time at farming and hunting like the other people of the village. He had often heard talk about the big town of Accra by the ocean, and all the wonderful things to be found there, but he had never seen it. He had never been farther from his village than the river.

But one day Younde had to go to Accra. He put on his best clothes, and took his knife and put it in his belt. He wrapped some food in a cloth and put it on his head and started out. He walked for many days, and the road was hot and dusty. After a while he was out of his own country, and people didn't speak Akim, which was his language, anymore. He came closer and closer to Accra. There were many people and donkeys on the way, all going to town or coming back from town, more people than he had ever seen on the road before.

Then he saw a great herd of cows **grazing** by the edge of the road. He had never seen so many cows in his life. He stopped and looked at them **in wonder**. He saw a little boy herding[1] the cows, and he went up to him and said, "Who is the owner of all these cattle?"

But the boy didn't understand Younde, because Younde spoke Akim, while in Accra they spoke the Ga language, and he replied,

---

1. *herding*: taking care of or moving along

"*Minu*," which meant "I don't understand."

"Minu! What a rich man he must be to own so many cows!" Younde said.

He continued on his way into the town. He was very **impressed** with everything he saw.

He came to a large building and stopped to look at it. It was made of stone, and it was very high. He shook his head. There was nothing like this back in the hills. When a woman came by on her way to market, Younde spoke to her.

"What a **tremendous** house!" he said. "What rich person can own such a building?"

But the woman didn't know what Younde was saying, because he talked Akim and she knew only Ga, so she replied to him, "Minu."[2]

"Minu! That man again!"

Younde was overcome. No one back in Akim had ever been so wealthy as Minu. As he went farther and farther into the town he kept seeing more wonders. He came to the market. It covered a space larger than all the houses in Younde's village. He walked through the center of it, and he saw the women selling things that were rare in his village, like iron pots and iron spoons.

"Where do all these things come from?" Younde asked a little girl.

She smiled at him.

"Minu," she replied.

Younde was silent. Everything was Minu. Minu everywhere.

---

2. *Minu*: This means "I don't understand" in the Ga language

CHECK YOUR READING

Put an **X** in the box next to the correct answer.

How many questions did you answer correctly? Circle your score. Then fill in your score on the Score Chart on page 190.

Number Correct	Score
1	10
2	20
3	30
4	40
5	50
6	60
7	70
8	80
9	90
10	100

Reading Comprehension

1. Younde lived in
   - ☐ **a.** the country of Akim.
   - ☐ **b.** a big town called Accra.
   - ☐ **c.** a city by the ocean.

2. Younde spent his time
   - ☐ **a.** farming and hunting.
   - ☐ **b.** working in a store.
   - ☐ **c.** teaching at a school.

3. When Younde went to Accra, he put on his
   - ☐ **a.** old clothes.
   - ☐ **b.** torn clothes.
   - ☐ **c.** best clothes.

4. When he got close to Accra, Younde saw
   - ☐ **a.** a friend of his from Akim.
   - ☐ **b.** only a few people.
   - ☐ **c.** more people than he had ever seen before.

5. Younde thought that *Minu*
   - ☐ **a.** meant "I don't understand."
   - ☐ **b.** was a rich man.
   - ☐ **c.** was a village.

6. The market in Accra was
   - ☐ **a.** very small.
   - ☐ **b.** very large.
   - ☐ **c.** as big as the market in Akim.

Vocabulary

7. There were some cows grazing by the edge of the road. The word *grazing* means
   - ☐ **a.** running around.
   - ☐ **b.** falling down.
   - ☐ **c.** eating grass.

8. Younde was very impressed with everything he saw. When you are *impressed* with something, you
   - ☐ **a.** don't see it.
   - ☐ **b.** don't care about it.
   - ☐ **c.** feel strongly about it.

9. When Younde saw a large building, he said, "What a tremendous house that is!" The word *tremendous* means
   - ☐ **a.** very great.
   - ☐ **b.** very weak.
   - ☐ **c.** very little.

Idioms

10. Since he had never been in Accra before, Younde looked at everything in wonder. The idiom *in wonder* means
    - ☐ **a.** in trouble.
    - ☐ **b.** in time.
    - ☐ **c.** in surprise.

UNDERSTANDING THE STORY

Exercise A ~ **Checking Comprehension**

Answer each question by writing a complete sentence. Begin each sentence with a capital letter, and end each sentence with a period. You may use the line numbers in parentheses to help you.

1. Where did Younde live? (1)

_____

2. How did Younde spend his time? (3)

_____

3. What did Younde put on when he went to Accra? (8)

_____

4. What did Younde wrap in a cloth? (10)

_____

5. How many people did Younde see on the road near Accra? (15)

_____

6. What language did the people in Accra speak? (23)

_____

7. What does *Minu* mean? (24)

_____

8. Describe (tell about) the large building that Younde saw. (29)

_____

9. How large was the market in Accra? (41)

_____

10. What were the women selling in the market? (42)

_____

Exercise B ~ Building Sentences

Make sentences by adding the correct letter.

1. _____ Younde had never gone

2. _____ He had heard people talk

3. _____ He walked for days along

4. _____ He saw many people going to or

5. _____ Younde had never seen so many

a. a hot, dusty road.

b. coming from Accra.

c. cows in his life.

d. far from his home.

e. about the town called Accra.

Now do questions 6–10 the same way.

6. _____ Younde saw a little boy who

7. _____ Younde thought that "Minu" was

8. _____ Younde spoke to a woman

9. _____ The woman didn't know what

10. _____ Younde asked a little girl where everything

a. Younde was saying.

b. was taking care of some cows.

c. came from.

d. who was going to the market.

e. a very rich man.

Now write the sentences on the lines below. Remember to begin each sentence with a capital letter and to end each sentence with a period.

1. _____

2. _____

3. _____

4. _____

5. _____

6. _____

7. _____

8. _____

9. _____

10. _____

Exercise C ~ Adding Vocabulary

In the box are 8 words from the story. Complete each sentence by adding the correct word.

herd	center	rare	wealthy
understand	language	silent	replied

1. Younde spoke Akim. That was his _____.

2. Younde saw a group of cows by the edge of the road. He looked at the

   _____.

3. The boy didn't know what Younde was saying. The boy didn't

   _____ him.

4. Younde walked until he came to the _____ of the village.

5. Younde asked the woman a question. "Minu," she _____.

6. Younde thought that Minu was very rich. No one in Akim was as

   _____ as Minu.

7. It was hard to find iron pots in Younde's village. They were

   _____.

8. Younde didn't say a word. He was _____.

Exercise D ~ Using Verbs Correctly

Change each positive sentence to a negative sentence by using *didn't* plus the correct form of the verb. The first one has been done for you.

1. Younde spent his time farming and hunting.

   *Younde **didn't spend** his time farming and hunting.*

2. Younde heard people talking about Accra.

   _____

3. Younde took his knife with him.

   _____

4. Younde walked for many days.

   _____

5. Younde saw a little boy.

   _____

6. Younde came to a large building.

   _____

7. Younde stopped to look at the cows.

   _____

8. Younde shook his head.

   _____

9. Younde spoke to the woman.

   _____

10. The woman knew what Younde was saying.

    _____

Exercise E ~ Adding Punctuation

The following passage needs punctuation marks. Add capital letters, periods, question marks, commas, and quotation marks. Then write the corrected passage on the lines below.

once there was a man named younde he lived in the country of akim one day he decided to visit the town of accra younde wrapped up some food and began to walk he walked for many days he saw cows donkeys people and a very large building younde asked a woman do you live in accra do you know who owns this building

Before You Read Part 2

Younde thinks that Minu is a very rich man. However, Minu is not the name of a man. *Minu* is a word that means "I don't understand." Do you think that Younde will learn the real meaning of *Minu*? See if you are right.

PART 2

The crowd was very great. People pushed and shoved, for it was the big market day and everyone within walking distance had come to sell or buy. Younde had never seen so many people in one place. The stories he had heard about Accra **hadn't done it**
5 **justice**. He stopped an old man with a drum under his arm and said, "So many people, all at one time! What makes so many people all come to Accra?"

"Minu,"[1] the old man said.

Younde was overwhelmed. What influence that Minu had! People
10 came to Accra in great crowds just because of him. How **ignorant** folks[2] back in the village were of this great person!

He went out of the market down to the ocean's edge. Lying in the water were many little fishing boats with sails, the first Younde had ever seen.

15 "Wah! To whom do all those boats belong?" he asked a fisherman standing on the beach.

"Minu," the fisherman replied.

Younde walked away, and came to where a large iron cargo ship was being loaded with palm oil and fruit. Smoke came out of its
20 stacks in huge black clouds, and hundreds of men swarmed[3] over its decks.

"Hah!" Younde said in great excitement to a man carrying a stalk of bananas on his head. "This must be the largest boat in the world!"

"Minu," the man said.

25 "Yes, I know. That much I guessed," Younde said. "But where is all the fruit going?"

"Minu," the man said, and went up onto the deck of the ship.

Younde was overcome. Minu was indeed a great man. He owned everything. He ate everything. You couldn't ask a question but
30 people would answer "Minu." Minu here, there, everywhere.

"I wouldn't have believed it if I hadn't seen it," Younde said.

---

1. *Minu*: This means "I don't understand" in the Ga language
2. *folks*: people
3. swarmed: moved or crowded together

"They ought to call Accra 'Minu's Town.' How wonderful it would be to have Minu's great wealth!"

Younde then transacted his business in Accra, and again he wrapped food in his cloth and set it on his head and started out for home.

When he came to the edge of the town, he saw a great procession[4] and heard the beating of drums. He came close and saw it was a funeral. Men were carrying a **coffin** and women were crying out in mourning[5]. It was the most impressive[6] funeral Younde had ever seen. He pushed his way into the crowd and looked. And to one of the mourners he said, "Who is this person who has died?"

And the mourner replied sadly, "Minu."

"What! The great Minu is dead?" Younde said. "The man who owned the cattle and the tall house, the sailing boats and the iron steamship? The man whose reputation has crowded the market place beyond belief? Oh, poor Minu! He had to leave all his wealth behind. He has died just like an ordinary person!"

Younde continued his way out of the city, but he couldn't get the **tragedy** of Minu from his mind.

"Poor Minu!" he said over and over again. "Poor Minu!"

4. *procession*: a large group of people moving forward

5. *mourning*: showing sadness at someone's death

6. *impressive*: something that affects a person very much

CHECK YOUR READING

Put an **X** in the box next to the correct answer.

Reading Comprehension

1. The crowd at Accra was very large because
- ☐ **a.** everyone was going to the movies.
- ☐ **b.** people were going home.
- ☐ **c.** it was the big market day.

2. Younde had never seen
- ☐ **a.** fishing boats.
- ☐ **b.** fishing boats with sails.
- ☐ **c.** people fishing.

3. Younde thought that the fishing boats belonged to
- ☐ **a.** a man named Minu.
- ☐ **b.** some of the fishermen.
- ☐ **c.** his friend.

4. The large iron ship was being loaded with
- ☐ **a.** palm oil and fruit.
- ☐ **b.** clothing.
- ☐ **c.** fish.

5. On his way home, Younde saw
- ☐ **a.** some friends from home.
- ☐ **b.** people at a funeral.
- ☐ **c.** Minu.

6. At the end of the story, Younde thought that Minu had
- ☐ **a.** just arrived at the village.
- ☐ **b.** spent all of his money.
- ☐ **c.** just died.

Vocabulary

7. People in Akim were ignorant of Minu. When you are *ignorant* of something, you
- ☐ **a.** know a lot about it.
- ☐ **b.** know everything about it.
- ☐ **c.** know little or nothing about it.

8. At the funeral, Younde saw some men carrying a coffin. A *coffin* is
- ☐ **a.** a bag filled with food.
- ☐ **b.** a box in which a dead person is buried.
- ☐ **c.** a small table.

9. Minu's death was a tragedy. The word *tragedy* means
- ☐ **a.** something happy.
- ☐ **b.** something strange.
- ☐ **c.** something terrible and sad.

Idioms

10. Accra was so wonderful, the stories about it *hadn't done it justice*. This means the stories
- ☐ **a.** took too long to tell.
- ☐ **b.** were very funny.
- ☐ **c.** didn't tell how great Accra really was.

UNDERSTANDING THE STORY

Exercise A ~ **Checking Comprehension**

Answer each question by writing a complete sentence. Begin each sentence with a capital letter, and end each sentence with a period. You may use the line numbers in parentheses to help you.

1. How big was the crowd on the market day? (1)

_____

2. What had everyone come to the market to do? (3)

_____

3. What did the old man that Younde stopped have under his arm? (5)

_____

4. What did Younde see in the water? (13)

_____

5. What was being loaded onto the large iron ship? (19)

_____

6. How many men were on the decks of the ship? (20)

_____

7. What did Younde think people should call Accra? (32)

_____

8. What did Younde think it would be wonderful to have? (32)

_____

9. After Younde wrapped his food in his cloth, where did he put it? (35)

_____

10. Why did Younde feel sad at the end of the story? (47)

_____

Exercise B ~ Building Sentences

Make sentences by adding the correct letter.

1. _____ At the market, everyone

2. _____ Younde thought people came to Accra

3. _____ Younde had never seen

4. _____ A man was carrying

5. _____ Younde thought it was the largest boat

a. bananas on his head.

b. pushed and shoved.

c. in the world.

d. because of Minu.

e. so many people.

Now do questions 6–10 the same way.

6. _____ A man went up onto

7. _____ At the edge of the town, Younde heard

8. _____ Younde pushed his way

9. _____ He thought that the great

10. _____ At the end of the story, Younde couldn't

a. stop thinking about Minu.

b. the deck of the ship.

c. the beating of drums.

d. into the crowd.

e. Minu had died.

Now write the sentences on the lines below. Remember to begin each sentence with a capital letter and to end each sentence with a period.

1. _____

2. _____

3. _____

4. _____

5. _____

6. _____

7. _____

8. _____

9. _____

10. _____

Exercise C ~ Adding Vocabulary

In the box are 8 words from the story. Complete each sentence by adding the correct word.

ordinary	reputation	transacted	distance
cargo	stacks	stalk	mourning

1. The _____ ship was being loaded with fruit.

2. Smoke came out of the ship's _____ in huge black clouds.

3. The man was carrying a _____ of bananas on his head.

4. Minu was very famous; everyone in the city had heard of his

   _____.

5. The wonderful Minu died just like an _____ person.

6. After Younde _____ his business, he went home to Akim.

7. Men and women were crying; they were _____ the person who had died.

8. Some people walked a great _____ to get to the market.

Exercise D ~ Using Verbs Correctly

Fill in the blanks in each sentence to form the **past perfect tense**. Write in the **past participle** of the verb in parentheses. The first one has been done for you.

1. Younde had _____*heard*_____ stories about Accra. (hear)

2. Younde had _____ to Accra to do business there. (go)

3. Younde had never _____ in Accra before. (be)

4. People in Akim had _____ about Accra. (speak)

5. Younde had never _____ so many people. (see)

6. The stories about Accra had not _____ it justice. (do)

7. Younde thought that Minu had _____ a large ship. (buy)

8. Minu had also _____ fruit and oil. (sell)

9. The great Minu had _____. (die)

10. He had _____ all his wealth behind. (leave)

Exercise E ~ Picking a Preposition

Fill in each blank by adding the correct preposition. Use each preposition once.

under	into	in	down
from	to	about	of

Remember, a **preposition** is a connecting word. It joins other words or groups of words.

preposition

Examples: Younde saw people *on* the boat.

preposition

Men and women walked *across* the street.

1. Younde had never been far _____ home.

2. He saw an old man who was carrying a drum _____ his arm.

3. Younde thought about the people who lived _____ his village.

4. After a while, Younde walked _____ to the ocean.

5. Younde pushed his way _____ the crowd.

6. While he was in Accra, Younde spoke _____ many people.

7. Younde finished his business and walked out _____ the city.

8. Younde couldn't stop thinking _____ the great Minu.

Write your own sentences using the prepositions in parentheses.

9. (with) _____

10. (up) _____

11. (above) _____

_____

12. (on) _____

_____

Exercise F ~ Vocabulary Review

Write a complete sentence for each word.

1. understood _____

_____

2. language _____

_____

3. wealthy _____

_____

4. grazing _____

_____

5. cargo _____

_____

6. mourning _____

_____

7. transacted _____

_____

8. distance _____

_____

9. coffin _____

_____

10. tragedy _____

_____

STUDYING THE STORY

A. Looking Back at the Story

Discuss these questions with your partner or with the group. Your teacher may ask you to write your answer to one of the questions.

■ How do you know that Younde's village was very small?

■ While he was in Accra, Younde asked people many questions. Think of another question that Younde might have asked someone in Accra. Tell the question and the answer.

■ Do you think the story had a sad ending or a funny ending? Explain why.

B. Charting Information in a Story

Suppose that Younde has returned to Akim. What do you think he might tell the people about Accra? Write one fact about Accra in each circle in the cluster map below. One fact has already been added. Do not write anything about Minu. You may look back at the story.

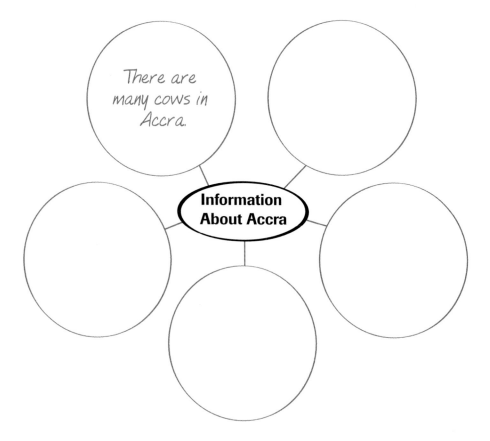

There are many cows in Accra.

Information About Accra

THINKING ABOUT LITERATURE

1. The word *folk* means "people," and the word *tale* means "story." Explain the meaning of the word *folktale*.

   _____

   _____

   _____

2. Often, animals are very important characters in **folktales**. In some African-American folktales, animals are the *only* characters in the story. Usually, these animals act in a certain way. For example, the rabbit and spider are very clever. They love to play tricks on the other animals. The lion is proud but greedy. The chicken is not very smart, and the lizard is often a thief.

   Pick two or three of those animals. Remember how they act. Then write a very short story about them. When you finish writing, you will have a story in the African-American folktale style.

   _____

   _____

   _____

   _____

   _____

   _____

   _____

   _____

   _____

   _____

   _____

FIRE

BY JACK LONDON

GETTING READY TO READ

1. The Story and You

The weather plays an important part in "Fire." How important is the weather to you? What kind of weather do you like best? Suppose that you had to live in a place that was very hot or very cold. Which one would you choose? Tell why.

2. Learning About Literature

In literature, the **setting** is the time and place of the action in a story—*where* and *when* the action takes place. Sometimes, *where* the action takes place can make the characters act in a certain way. The *setting* can also give the story a special feeling, or *mood*. Notice how important the setting is in "Fire."

3. Looking Ahead

Look at the picture on the left. Tell how the man is dressed. Where do you think the story might take place? Think about the title of the story. What do you think will probably happen? Read on to see if you are right.

FIRE

BY JACK LONDON

PART 1

The day was cold and gray, **extremely** cold and gray when the man turned off the main Yukon[1] trail and climbed up a path that went up a high hill. At the top, he paused to look at his watch. It was nine o'clock. He had been up for two hours.

5 　There was no sun in the sky, although there was not a cloud anywhere. It had been days since he had seen the sun, but that did not worry the man. Although he was a newcomer to the land, he knew about the Yukon and how it was there.

　The man looked back along the path he had come. The trail was
10 hidden under several feet of ice and snow. Everything was pure white for as far as he could see.

　The man continued to walk. It was colder than fifty below, but the temperature did not matter to him. He was heading for the camp beyond Henderson Creek. The other men were already there. He had
15 gone by himself to **check out** some lumber land he wanted to buy. He **calculated** that he would get to the camp around six o'clock. There would be a fire going and the men would have supper ready for him.

　He thought of food, and he pressed his hand against the bundle under his jacket. He had some bread wrapped in a handkerchief under
20 his shirt. That was the only way to keep the bread from freezing.

　At the man's heels trotted a big, gray dog, a husky. It was unhappy about the terrible cold. The dog did not know that it was actually seventy-five degrees below zero. But it knew that it was no time for traveling. The dog expected the man to go into a camp or to seek shelter
25 and build a fire. The dog had learned about fire, and it wanted fire.

　The man walked for several miles until he came to a small, frozen stream. He began to walk along the top of the frozen stream. The dog followed, its tail drooping. The man was very careful where he placed his feet. The stream was frozen, but he knew that there were springs
30 that bubbled under the snow. These springs never froze, no matter how cold it got. They were traps that held pools of water under the snow. The water might be three inches deep or three feet deep.

---

1. *Yukon:* a part of Canada that has very long, cold winters

The man knew that if his feet got wet, they would quickly freeze. He would have to stop and build a fire. He would have to take off his boots and socks and dry off near the flames. So the man walked carefully, and he studied the top of the stream as he looked for the hidden traps. Once he had a close call. He felt the ice breaking under his feet. He heard a loud snapping sound, and he jumped away just in time.

Another time, he **suspected** danger. To test the ice, he pushed the dog forward. Suddenly there was a loud crack, and the dog nearly fell through the ice. The dog jumped to one side and landed safely.

But one foot had gotten wet and ice immediately[2] began to form on the animal's paw. The dog licked off the ice. Then the dog dropped down in the snow and quickly bit off the ice from between its toes.

The man decided it was time to have something to eat. He put his hand under his jacket and shirt and pulled out the bread. Then he sat down on a snow-covered log. He put the bread up to his face, but he could not eat. Ice had formed around his beard and covered his face. The man smiled at his foolishness. He had forgotten to build a fire to thaw himself out.

Just then, he noticed a sharp stinging in his toes. He tried to move his toes, but they refused to move. He stood up and stamped up and down until a warm feeling returned to his feet.

That old-timer[3] from Sulphur Creek had told the truth when he said how cold it got in the Yukon. The man hadn't believed the old-timer then. He had laughed at him. The old-timer had said there was a rule about traveling in the Yukon. He said you must never travel alone in the Yukon when it was fifty below.

Well, he was traveling alone. He would be okay. But he must build a fire now.

2. *immediately:* right away, now

3. *old-timer:* someone who has lived at a place for a long time

CHECK YOUR READING

Put an **X** in the box next to the correct answer.

How many questions did you answer correctly? Circle your score. Then fill in your score on the Score Chart on page 190.

Number Correct	Score
1	10
2	20
3	30
4	40
5	50
6	60
7	70
8	80
9	90
10	100

Reading Comprehension

1. The man had not seen the sun for
   - ☐ **a.** days.
   - ☐ **b.** a few weeks.
   - ☐ **c.** about a year.

2. The trail was hidden under
   - ☐ **a.** bushes and trees.
   - ☐ **b.** piles of earth.
   - ☐ **c.** ice and snow.

3. The man had some bread
   - ☐ **a.** in his pocket.
   - ☐ **b.** in his jacket.
   - ☐ **c.** under his shirt.

4. The dog expected the man to
   - ☐ **a.** walk all day and all night.
   - ☐ **b.** build a fire.
   - ☐ **c.** wait for help.

5. The man was worried about
   - ☐ **a.** getting his feet wet.
   - ☐ **b.** finding food for the dog.
   - ☐ **c.** arriving at the camp too early.

6. The man could not eat the bread because
   - ☐ **a.** he lost it on the trail.
   - ☐ **b.** ice covered his face.
   - ☐ **c.** the bread was too hard.

Vocabulary

7. The day was extremely cold and gray. The word *extremely* means
   - ☐ **a.** never.
   - ☐ **b.** almost.
   - ☐ **c.** very.

8. The man calculated that he would get to the camp around six o'clock. The word *calculated* means
   - ☐ **a.** thought or figured out.
   - ☐ **b.** became scared or afraid.
   - ☐ **c.** sent a letter or message.

9. When the man suspected danger, he pushed the dog forward. The word *suspected* means
   - ☐ **a.** didn't care about.
   - ☐ **b.** thought that something was going to happen.
   - ☐ **c.** forgot about everything.

Idioms

10. He was going to check out some land he wanted to buy. The idiom *check out* means
    - ☐ **a.** forget about.
    - ☐ **b.** find out about.
    - ☐ **c.** say nothing about

UNDERSTANDING THE STORY

Exercise A ~ Checking Comprehension

Answer each question by writing a complete sentence. Begin each sentence with a capital letter, and end each sentence with a period. You may use the line numbers in parentheses to help you.

1. What kind of day was it? (1)

_____

2. How long had it been since the man had seen the sun? (6)

_____

3. Where was the man going? (13)

_____

4. When did the man think he would get to the camp? (16)

_____

5. How cold was it actually? (23)

_____

6. What would the man have to do if his feet got wet? (34)

_____

7. What did the dog do when ice formed between its toes? (44)

_____

8. Why couldn't the man eat the bread? (48)

_____

9. How did the man get feeling to return to his feet? (52)

_____

10. What was the rule about traveling in the Yukon? (57)

_____

Exercise B ~ Building Sentences

Make sentences by adding the correct letter.

1. _____ The man paused to

a. wrapped in a handkerchief.

2. _____ He had some bread

b. look at his watch.

3. _____ The dog was unhappy about

c. breaking under his feet.

4. _____ The man walked on the top of

d. the terrible cold.

5. _____ He felt the ice

e. a frozen stream.

Now do questions 6-10 the same way.

6. _____ There were pools of water

a. a snow-covered log.

7. _____ The dog nearly

b. build a fire.

8. _____ The man sat down on

c. fell through the ice.

9. _____ The man noticed a sharp stinging

d. under the snow.

10. _____ The man had to stop to

e. in his toes.

Now write the sentences on the lines below. Remember to begin each sentence with a capital letter and to end each sentence with a period.

1. _____

2. _____

3. _____

4. _____

5. _____

6. _____

7. _____

8. _____

9. _____

10. _____

Exercise C ～ Adding Vocabulary

In the box are 8 words from the story. Complete each sentence by adding the correct word.

foolishness	seek	thaw	drooping
paused	degrees	temperature	newcomer

1. The man stopped on the hill. He _____ to look at his watch.

2. He had not been in the Yukon very long. He was a

   _____ to the land.

3. The dog knew it was too cold to travel, but the man did not care what

   the _____ was.

4. It was even colder than he realized. It was seventy-five

   _____ below zero.

5. The dog hoped that the man would _____ shelter from the cold.

6. The animal moved along slowly and unhappily. Its tail was

   _____.

7. He knew he had been silly, and he smiled at his

   _____.

8. Ice covered the man's beard and his face. He had to build a fire to

   _____ himself out.

Exercise D ~ Picking an Adjective

Fill in each blank by adding the correct adjective from the box. Use each adjective once.

heavy	terrible	sad	frightened
high	frozen	long	wise

Remember, an **adjective** is a word that describes (tells about) a noun.

adjective

Example: It was a *cold* day.

1. He climbed up a path that went up a _____ hill.

2. The path ran for many miles. It was a very _____ path.

3. The dog did not want to travel in the _____ cold.

4. The man was wearing a thick, _____ jacket.

5. He walked carefully on the top of a small, _____ stream.

6. When the ice cracked, the _____ animal jumped back quickly.

7. The man was brave, but he was not _____.

8. Will the story have a _____ ending or a happy ending?

Write your own sentences using the adjective in parentheses.

9. (tired) _____

10. (huge) _____

Exercise E ~ True or False?

Part A

Write **T** if the statement is true. Write **F** if the statement is false.

1. _____ It was a warm, sunny day.

2. _____ The man was a newcomer to the land.

3. _____ The man had a piece of cake wrapped under his shirt.

4. _____ The dog didn't know about fire.

5. _____ The man didn't want his feet to get wet.

6. _____ The dog nearly fell through the ice.

7. _____ The man jumped up and down to keep his feet warm.

8. _____ The man decided not to build a fire.

Part B

On the lines below, correct the four false statements.

a. _____

b. _____

c. _____

d. _____

Before You Read Part 2

The man is on his way to the camp beyond Henderson Creek. He has been told that he must never travel alone in the Yukon when it is fifty below. It is even colder than that, but he thinks he will be all right. Do you think that the man will arrive safely at the camp? See if you are right.

PART 2

The man began to search for wood. Near the stream, he found a pile of twigs. Then he **proceeded** to make a fire. He worked carefully, and soon he had a roaring flame going. He thawed the ice from his face and was able to eat the bread. The dog crept close to the fire and felt satisfied.

The man rested for a few minutes. Then he stood up and set out again. The dog was disappointed. It wanted to stay near the fire. It knew that it was not good to walk about in such fierce cold. The man whistled to the dog. The dog looked back at the fire, and then it obeyed the man and trotted toward him.

The man walked quickly because there did not seem to be so many springs here. Then it happened. At a place where there were no signs of a spring, the man broke through the ice and found himself in water up to his knees.

The man scrambled to dry ground, angrily. This would delay him for an hour. He would have to build a fire to get dry.
On top of a little hill, he saw a few spruce trees. He rushed to the trees, pulled off some branches, and threw them down on the snow by the tree. Then he got matches from his pocket and started a fire.

As the flames grew stronger, he added more branches from the tree. He knew there must be no **failure** because it was very cold and his feet were wet.

Finally the fire was crackling and snapping. He was safe.

The man smiled as he remembered the old-timer at Sulphur Creek. The old-timer had said that you must never travel alone in the Yukon at fifty below. Well, here he was. He had had an accident, but he had saved himself. He laughed at the old-timer. As long as a man didn't **lose his head**, he was all right.

Just then, the man heard a dull sound. He saw snow falling from the trees onto the fire. He should have built the fire out in the open, not under the trees. He had been shaking the tree before. Now piles of snow poured down from the trees onto the man and onto the fire.

The man stared at the fire. It was out.

The man was shocked. It was as though he had just heard his own
death sentence. He stared in horror at the spot where the fire had
been. Then he became very calm. He would have to build the fire
over again out in the open.

He gathered twigs and branches. It was very hard work because
his fingers felt stiff, and he had difficulty moving them.

When everything was ready, the man reached into his pocket for
the matches. He knew that they were there, but he could not feel
them with his fingers. He beat his hands against his sides until there
was some feeling in his fingers. He pulled off a glove, reached into
his pocket, and pulled out the matches. Suddenly, the cold hit his
hand and his fingers went dead. The matches dropped into the snow.

The man reached down and tried to pick them up, but he was
unable to do so. Suddenly, **panic** hit the man. He heard the ice on
his beard snap and his feet were freezing. He began to run wildly,
blindly, up the trail with the dog following him.

Suddenly, the man's legs gave out and he fell in the snow. The
man thought to himself, "Old-timer, you were right."

Then the man **drowsed** off into the best sleep he had ever had.
The dog sat facing him and waited. It had never known a man to sit
like that in the snow and not make a fire.

The dog whined loudly. It crept close to the man and smelled the
scent of death. The dog jumped up, backed away, and waited a while.
Then it turned and trotted in the direction of the camp it knew.
There were other men there who could build a fire.

Read the last paragraph of the story again. What can you infer, or
figure out, has happened to the man? Which sentence gives you the
information you need to figure this out? When you **draw an
inference**, you use clues or facts in the story to reach a decision.

Meet the Author

Jack London (1876–1916) was born in California. He traveled around the world and lived a very exciting life. Before he was 17 years old, he had visited Japan and China. In 1897, London went to the Yukon. His experiences there helped him write *The Call of the Wild* and *White Fang*, two famous novels. Many of London's stories take place in the Yukon, which is the setting of the story "Fire."

CHECK YOUR READING

Put an **X** in the box next to the correct answer.

Reading Comprehension

1. The dog did not want to
- ☐ **a.** stay near the fire.
- ☐ **b.** walk in the cold.
- ☐ **c.** stop to rest.

2. The man built a fire to
- ☐ **a.** dry himself and his clothes.
- ☐ **b.** help the dog get warm.
- ☐ **c.** cook the food he had brought.

3. The fire went out because
- ☐ **a.** the dog kicked snow into the fire.
- ☐ **b.** the fire needed more wood.
- ☐ **c.** snow fell onto the fire.

4. At the end of the story, the man couldn't pick up the matches because
- ☐ **a.** he couldn't find them in the snow.
- ☐ **b.** the matches were too heavy.
- ☐ **c.** his fingers were frozen.

5. At the end of the story, the dog
- ☐ **a.** went to find a camp and other men.
- ☐ **b.** did not leave the man.
- ☐ **c.** died in the snow.

Vocabulary

6. He found some twigs and proceeded to make a fire. The word *proceeded* means
- ☐ **a.** stopped.
- ☐ **b.** wondered about.
- ☐ **c.** kept on going.

7. The man knew that failure to build a fire could cost him his life. The word *failure* means
- ☐ **a.** doing something very well.
- ☐ **b.** being unable to do something.
- ☐ **c.** asking others for help.

8. When the man could not pick up the matches, he was filled with panic. The word *panic* means
- ☐ **a.** terrible fear.
- ☐ **b.** happiness or joy.
- ☐ **c.** hunger.

9. He drowsed off into sleep. The word *drowsed* means
- ☐ **a.** dreamed for an hour.
- ☐ **b.** became sleepy.
- ☐ **c.** woke up.

Idioms

10. He thought he would be all right as long as he didn't lose his head. The idiom *lose his head* means
- ☐ **a.** to become too excited to think clearly.
- ☐ **b.** to stay calm.
- ☐ **c.** to look for trouble.

How many questions did you answer correctly? Circle your score. Then fill in your score on the Score Chart on page 190.

Number Correct	Score
1	10
2	20
3	30
4	40
5	50
6	60
7	70
8	80
9	90
10	100

UNDERSTANDING THE STORY

Exercise A ~ Checking Comprehension

Answer each question by writing a complete sentence. Begin each sentence with a capital letter, and end each sentence with a period. You may use the line numbers in parentheses to help you.

1. What did the man find near the stream? (1)

_____

2. Why was the dog disappointed? (7)

_____

3. What happened when the man broke through the ice? (13)

_____

4. What did the man pull off the spruce trees? (18)

_____

5. Where should the man have built the fire? (30)

_____

6. What poured down onto the man and the fire? (32)

_____

7. Why couldn't the man take the matches out of his pocket? (41)

_____

8. What did the man think to himself when he fell in the snow? (51)

_____

9. What did the dog smell when it crept close to the man? (55)

_____

10. Where did the dog go? (57)

_____

Exercise B ~ Building Sentences

Make sentences by adding the correct letter.

1. _____ The man started a fire with   **a.** the old-timer told him.

2. _____ The dog crept   **b.** and landed in water.

3. _____ The man broke through the ice   **c.** close to the fire.

4. _____ The man's feet were cold because   **d.** a pile of twigs.

5. _____ The man remembered what   **e.** they were wet.

Now do questions 6-10 the same way.

6. _____ Building a fire was hard because   **a.** waited for a while.

7. _____ The matches dropped   **b.** who could build a fire.

8. _____ The man knew that the   **c.** old-timer was right.

9. _____ The dog backed away and   **d.** the man's fingers were stiff.

10. _____ There were other men   **e.** into the snow.

Now write the sentences on the lines below. Remember to begin each sentence with a capital letter and to end each sentence with a period.

1. _____

2. _____

3. _____

4. _____

5. _____

6. _____

7. _____

8. _____

9. _____

10. _____

Exercise C ~ Adding Vocabulary

In the box are 8 words from the story. Complete each sentence by adding the correct word. Use each word once.

crackling	scrambled	horror	delay
whined	obeyed	satisfied	scent

1. The dog was very pleased to see the fire. He crept close to the flames

   and was _____.

2. The man whistled to the dog. The dog _____ the
   man and trotted toward him.

3. After the man broke through the ice, he quickly got out of the water and

   _____ to dry ground.

4. He wanted to get to the camp by six o'clock, but he knew that falling

   through the ice would _____ him for an hour.

5. He added branches to the flames, and soon the fire was

   _____ and snapping.

6. The man was shocked. He stared in _____ at the
   spot where the fire had been.

7. The dog was surprised that the man did not move. The dog raised its

   head and _____ loudly.

8. The dog came close to the man and smelled the

   _____ of death.

Exercise D ~ Picking an Adverb

Fill in each blank by adding the correct adverb form the box. Use each adverb once.

loudly	happily	wildly	calmly
slowly	suddenly	foolishly	quickly

Remember, an **adverb** usually describes (tells about) a verb.
Adverbs often end with the letters *ly*.

verb   adverb

Example: The man *shouted angrily*.

1. The man was tired, so he walked _____.

2. The dog barked _____, but no one heard its cries.

3. He did not know where he was going, and he began to run

   _____.

4. Without any warning, piles of snow _____ fell on the man.

5. The dog saw the ice start to crack, so it _____ jumped to a safe spot.

6. The old-timer probably thought that the man was acting

   _____.

7. When you are in a lot of trouble, it is hard to act

   _____.

8. It was a sad story. It did not end _____.

Write your own sentences using the adverbs in parentheses.

9. (wisely) _____

10. (sadly) _____

Exercise E ~ Putting Words in Order

Unscramble each sentence by putting the words in the correct order. Write each sentence on the line. Each sentence is in the **present tense**.

1. takes / place /Yukon / story / This / the / in

_____

2. story / is / the / Who /writer / this / of

_____

3. traveler's / tells / story /a / about / The / adventures

_____

4. camp / tries / reach / to / He / a / away / miles

_____

5. follows / dog / man / the / A

_____

6. knows / The / he / fire / build / man / a / must

_____

7. fire / snow / He / a / the / makes / in

_____

8. out / fire / the / goes / man / The / dies / and

_____

Exercise F ~ Vocabulary Review

Write a complete sentence for each word or group of words.

1. temperature _____

_____

2. newcomer _____

_____

3. calculated _____

_____

4. thaw _____

_____

5. seek _____

_____

6. delay _____

_____

7. proceeded _____

_____

8. horror _____

_____

9. scent _____

_____

10. lose his head _____

_____

STUDYING THE STORY

A. Looking Back at the Story

Discuss these questions with your partner or with the group. Your teacher may ask you to write your answer to one of the questions.

- Why did the man walk very carefully on top of the frozen stream?

- Why was the dog unhappy with the man?

- What were three mistakes that the man made?

- Show that nature plays a very important part in the story.

B. Using a Chart to Put Events in Correct Order

Below are some events that took place in "Fire." Use the chart to put the events in the order in which they happened. Write the correct letter in each box. The first one has been done for you. You may look back at the story.

a. The man ran blindly up the trail and fell in the snow.

b. The man broke through the ice and fell in water up to his knees.

c. The man climbed up a path and headed toward the camp beyond Henderson Creek.

d. The dog waited, and then it trotted in the direction of a camp it knew.

e. Snow fell down from the trees onto the man and onto the fire.

f. The man pulled branches off some spruce trees and started a fire.

g. The man saw that the fire was out.

THINKING ABOUT LITERATURE

1. The **main character** is the person the story is mostly about. It is easy to tell that the traveler is the *main character* in "Fire." On the lines below, write three important facts about the man.

   a. _____

   _____

   b. _____

   _____

   c. _____

   _____

2. "Fire" takes place in the icy, frozen Yukon. You can see why the **setting** is so important to the story. Think of an interesting setting for a story of your own. For example, your story might be set somewhere on a desert island, on a strange planet, or at the top of a high, rocky mountain. If you wish, think of some other unusual place.

   Write the beginning of your story. Be sure to describe the setting fully.

   _____

   _____

   _____

   _____

   _____

   _____

   _____

   _____

   _____

   _____

Dr. Heidegger's Experiment

by Nathaniel Hawthorne

Getting Ready to Read

1. The Story and You

In this story, you will meet Dr. Heidegger, a scientist who liked to do experiments. As you know, experiments can lead to important discoveries. Think of some great scientific discoveries that have been made. Which one do you think was the greatest discovery of all? Explain why.

2. Learning About Literature

You know that the *plot* tells the important events in a story. The **theme** of a story is different from the plot. The *theme* is the *main idea* of the story. Ask yourself, "What is the main point, or main idea, the writer is making?" That is the theme. Try to find the theme in "Dr. Heidegger's Experiment."

3. Looking Ahead

Look closely at the picture on the left. What is the biggest difference between the characters at the top of the page and the characters at the bottom? When does the story take place? How do you know? Notice the four glasses in the picture. What do you think might be in the glasses? Think about the title of the story before you answer this question. Read on to see if you are right.

DR. HEIDEGGER'S EXPERIMENT

BY NATHANIEL HAWTHORNE

PART 1

DR. Heidegger was a strange old man. Once, he invited four friends to meet with him at his house. Three of his guests were old men with white beards. Their names were Mr. Medbourne, Mr. Gascon, and Colonel Killigrew. The fourth person was
5 an elderly woman with white hair. She was called the Widow Wycherly.

All of these people had lived very sad and **unfortunate** lives.

Years ago Mr. Medbourne had been a rich man. But because he was greedy[1], he made some bad business deals and lost his fortune. Now he had to beg for money.

10 Mr. Gascon had been a famous politician. But he was dishonest. He was caught stealing money and was sent to jail. Now he was poor and lived in shame.

Colonel Killigrew was once a great soldier. But he spent his life eating and drinking too much. Now his health was bad, and he was
15 sick all the time.

As for the Widow Wycherly, she was once quite beautiful. But she was very conceited[2]. She thought that she was the most beautiful woman in the town. She was not beautiful now.

The three men had each loved her very much when they were
20 young. Once, they almost killed each other fighting over her. But that was many years ago.

"My dear old friends," said Dr. Heidegger, "please come with me to my laboratory[3]. I need your help with a little experiment." Dr. Heidegger showed them the way.

---

1. *greedy:* always wanting more money or things
2. *conceited:* to think very highly of oneself
3. *laboratory:* a room where a scientist works

25   Dr. Heidegger's laboratory was certainly an unusual place. It was a large, dark room covered with spider webs and dust. Around the walls stood tall wooden bookcases that were filled with books. Between two of the bookcases there was a large painting of a young woman in a long silk dress. More than fifty years ago, Dr. Heidegger

30   was going to marry this woman. The day before their wedding, she suddenly became ill. Dr. Heidegger gave her some medicine, but she died that evening. Some people said that Dr. Heidegger made a mistake and gave her the wrong medicine.

    "My dear old friends," repeated Dr. Heidegger, "may I **count on**

35   your help with my little experiment?"

    Dr. Heidegger did not wait for an answer. He walked slowly across the room to one of the bookcases. He opened a book and removed a rose from its pages. Yes, it was a rose—or what once was a rose. The red flower had turned brown and seemed ready to **crumble** to dust

40   in the doctor's hands.

    Dr. Heidegger said, "Fifty-five years ago this rose was given to me by the woman I wanted to marry. Her name was Sylvia Ward. You can see her picture hanging there on the wall. I was going to wear this rose in my jacket on our wedding day."

45   Dr. Heidegger looked at his guests and said, "For fifty-five years I have saved this rose between the pages of a book. For fifty-five years I have treasured this rose." Dr. Heidegger asked suddenly, "Do you think that this old rose could ever bloom again?"

    "No, never," said the Widow Wycherly. "You might as well ask if

50   an old woman's wrinkled face could ever be young again."

    "Watch!" said Dr. Heidegger.

    They were sitting around a table. In the middle of the table was a large glass vase. It was filled with a liquid that looked like water. There were also four glasses on the table.

55   Dr. Heidegger picked up the vase. He poured some of the water onto the rose. At first nothing happened. But then the old, dried-out

rose began to bloom. The rose turned red. A moment later, it looked as fresh and lovely as it did fifty-five years ago.

The doctor's friends smiled and clapped their hands.

60 "That was a wonderful trick," said Mr. Gascon. "How did you do it?"

"My friends," said Dr. Heidegger, "that was no trick. Have you ever heard of the 'Fountain of Youth'?"

"The Fountain of Youth!" exclaimed Mr. Gascon.

"Yes," said Dr. Heidegger. "The water from that fountain makes
65 everything young again. Ponce de Leon, the Spanish explorer, searched for the fountain centuries ago."

"Did he ever find it?" asked the Widow Wycherly.

"No," answered Dr. Heidegger. "He was not looking in the right place. I have learned that the fountain is hidden in a forest near Lake
70 Macaco in the southern part of Florida."

Dr. Heidegger's guests were astonished[4] and looked at each other in surprise.

"A friend of mine," said Dr. Heidegger, "knows that I am interested in things like this. He sent me some water from the
75 fountain. It is here in this vase."

Colonel Killigrew coughed softly. He smiled and shook his head. He did not believe a word of the doctor's story. The Colonel stared at the vase and then asked, "But tell me this, doctor. What would happen if a person drank that water?"

80 "You shall see for yourself," said Dr. Heidegger. "Yes, all of you shall see."

Dr. Heidegger pointed to the vase. "My friends," he said, "you may drink as much of this water as you wish. Grow as young as you want to be. As for me, it took me a long time to grow old. I am in no
85 hurry to grow young again. I will be happy just to watch."

---

4. *astonished:* surprised

CHECK YOUR READING

Put an **X** in the box next to the correct answer.

Vocabulary

1. Dr. Heidegger invited
   - ☐ **a.** four friends to his home.
   - ☐ **b.** five friends to his home.
   - ☐ **c.** six friends to his home.

2. The Widow Wycherly was once
   - ☐ **a.** very rich.
   - ☐ **b.** very fat.
   - ☐ **c.** very beautiful.

3. What was between two bookcases in Dr. Heidegger's laboratory?
   - ☐ **a.** a window
   - ☐ **b.** a painting
   - ☐ **c.** a mirror

4. Dr. Heidegger took a rose from
   - ☐ **a.** the pages of a book.
   - ☐ **b.** his garden.
   - ☐ **c.** a vase.

5. Dr. Heidegger had the rose for
   - ☐ **a.** twenty-five years.
   - ☐ **b.** thirty-five years.
   - ☐ **c.** fifty-five years.

6. Dr. Heidegger said that the Fountain of Youth was in
   - ☐ **a.** Spain.
   - ☐ **b.** Florida.
   - ☐ **c.** California.

7. Who sent Dr. Heidegger some water from the Fountain?
   - ☐ **a.** Ponce de Leon
   - ☐ **b.** Mr. Gascon
   - ☐ **c.** a friend

Vocabulary

8. All of them had lived very sad and unfortunate lives. The word *unfortunate* means
   - ☐ **a.** not lucky.
   - ☐ **b.** very happy.
   - ☐ **c.** very short.

9. The old rose seemed ready to crumble to dust. The verb *to crumble* means
   - ☐ **a.** to get bigger.
   - ☐ **b.** to get brighter.
   - ☐ **c.** to break into small pieces.

Idioms

10. Dr. Heidegger asked his friends if he could count on their help. The idiom *count on* means
    - ☐ **a.** to count how many.
    - ☐ **b.** to depend on or rely on.
    - ☐ **c.** to forget about.

How many questions did you answer correctly? Circle your score. Then fill in your score on the Score Chart on page 190.

Number Correct	Score
1	10
2	20
3	30
4	40
5	50
6	60
7	70
8	80
9	90
10	100

UNDERSTANDING THE STORY

Exercise A ~ Checking Comprehension

Answer each question by writing a complete sentence. Begin each sentence with a capital letter, and end each sentence with a period. You may use the line numbers in parentheses to help you.

1. Who was Dr. Heidegger? (1)

_____

2. How had Colonel Killigrew spent his life? (13)

_____

3. What was between two bookcases in Dr. Heidegger's laboratory? (28)

_____

4. What did Dr. Heidegger remove from the pages of a book? (38)

_____

5. For how many years had Dr. Heidegger saved the rose? (45)

_____

6. What was in the middle of the table? (52)

_____

7. How many glasses were on the table? (54)

_____

8. What happened to the old rose after Dr. Heidegger poured water on it? (56)

_____

9. Who searched for the Fountain of Youth? (65)

_____

10. Who sent Dr. Heidegger some water from the fountain? (73)

_____

Exercise B ~ Building Sentences

Make sentences by adding the correct letter.

1. _____ Three of the guests were   **a.** filled with books.

2. _____ The three men once   **b.** old men.

3. _____ The tall bookcases were   **c.** in his jacket.

4. _____ The doctor gave her medicine, but **d.** loved the Widow Wycherly.

5. _____ The doctor was going to wear the rose   **e.** she died that evening.

Now do questions 6–10 the same way.

6. _____ They were all sitting   **a.** some water onto the rose.

7. _____ Dr. Heidegger poured   **b.** clapped their hands.

8. _____ The doctor's friends   **c.** around a table.

9. _____ The Colonel did not believe   **d.** to grow old.

10. _____ It took the doctor a long time   **e.** the doctor's story.

Now write the sentences on the lines below. Remember to begin each sentence with a capital letter and to end each sentence with a period.

1. _____

2. _____

3. _____

4. _____

5. _____

6. _____

7. _____

8. _____

9. _____

10. _____

Exercise C ~ Adding Vocabulary

In the box are 8 words from the story. Complete each sentence by adding the correct word.

liquid	fortune	dishonest	centuries
wrinkled	spider	conceited	astonished

1. Mr. Medbourne was once rich, but he lost his _____.

2. Mr. Gascon was _____ and was caught stealing money.

3. The Widow Wycherly was in love with her own beauty; she was very

   _____.

4. Dr. Heidegger's laboratory was covered with _____ webs and dust.

5. The old woman's _____ face was no longer young.

6. The vase was filled with a _____ that looked like water.

7. Dr. Heidegger's friends were _____ and looked at each other in surprise.

8. An explorer searched for the fountain _____ ago.

Exercise D ~ Changing Statements to Questions

Change each statement to a question that begins with *Who*. Put a question mark at the end of each question. The first one has been done for you.

1. Dr. Heidegger invited some friends to his house.

   Who invited some friends to his house?

2. Mr. Medbourne was once a rich man.

   _____

3. Mr. Gascon was sent to jail for stealing money.

   _____

4. Colonel Killigrew spent his life eating and drinking too much.

   _____

5. The Widow Wycherly was once very beautiful.

   _____

6. The three men loved the Widow Wycherly many years ago.

   _____

7. Sylvia Ward was going to marry Dr. Heidegger.

   _____

8. The Spanish explorer, Ponce de Leon, searched for the Fountain of Youth.

   _____

9. A friend sent Dr. Heidegger some water from the fountain.

   _____

10. Nathaniel Hawthorne wrote the story "Dr. Heidegger's Experiment."

   _____

Exercise E ~ Comparing Adjectives and Adverbs

The following chart shows the comparison of some adjectives and adverbs. Use the chart to help you fill in the blanks in the sentences below. The first one has been done for you.

Positive	Comparative	Superlative
rich	richer	richest
beautiful	more beautiful	most beautiful
(irregular) bad	worse	worst

1. Mr. Medbourne once had a lot of money. He was ___rich___ .

2. The Widow Wycherly had more money than Mr. Medbourne. She was

   _____ than Mr. Medbourne.

3. Dr. Heidegger had the most money. He was the _____
   person there.

4. Colonel Killigrew was sick. His health was _____ .

5. Mr. Gascon was sicker than the Widow Wycherly. His health was

   _____ than hers.

6. Mr. Medbourne was very, very ill. He had the _____ health
   of anyone.

7. The Widow Wycherly loved to look in the mirror. She thought that she

   was the _____ woman in town.

Before You Read Part 2

At the end of Part 1, Dr. Heidegger offered four sad, old friends a drink from the Fountain of Youth. Suppose they decide to drink the water. Do you think that the water really will make them young? If they do become young, do you think they will be happy? See if you are right.

PART 2

While he was speaking, Dr. Heidegger had been filling the four glasses with water from the Fountain of Youth. The water sparkled with bubbles and had a very sweet smell. The old people were eager to drink the water at once.

5 "Wait!" said Dr. Heidegger. "Wait! Before you drink, think about the mistakes you made when you were young. You would not want to make the same mistakes again."

"Of course not!" said Colonel Killigrew. "Of course not!" said the others. They all agreed that if they could live their lives over, they
10 would be better people.

"Drink then," said the doctor. "I am very glad that I selected you for my experiment."

With **trembling** hands, the four people raised the glasses to their lips. They drank.

15 A moment later, they noticed a change. They felt happier and better. The Widow Wycherly put her hands up to her head and adjusted her hat. She was beginning to feel like a young woman again.

"Give us more of this wonderful water!" they cried. "We are
20 younger, that is true! But we are still too old! Quick, give us more!"

"What is your hurry?" said Dr. Heidegger. "It took you many years to grow old. Surely, you can wait a few more minutes to grow young. But I will give you more water."

Dr. Heidegger filled their glasses again. The four guests quickly
25 drank the liquid. Then—could it be true? Their eyes grew bright and clear. Their white hair grew dark. They were now three men who were middle-aged—not old—and a young woman.

"My dear widow, you are beautiful again!" cried Colonel Killigrew. He was staring at her face.

30 The widow knew that Colonel Killigrew did not always tell the truth. She jumped up and ran to the mirror to look at herself. She was afraid that she would see deep lines in her face.

Meanwhile, the three men were acting in a very strange way. Mr. Gascon had climbed up on a chair. He was waving his arms like a politician. "Vote for me!" he was shouting. "Vote for me! Vote for me!"

Colonel Killigrew was singing loudly. At the same time, he was thinking about dinner. He was imagining plates piled with food and glasses filled with wine. On the other side of the table, Mr. Medbourne was figuring out a shrewd business deal that would make him rich.

As for the Widow Wycherly, she stood in front of the mirror and kept smiling at her face. It was like meeting a lost friend; a friend she loved more than anything in the world.

Finally, she turned away from the mirror and skipped over to Dr. Heidegger.

"My dear doctor," she said, "may I have another glass?"

"Certainly," said Dr. Heidegger. "See. I have already filled four more glasses."

There, in fact, stood the four glasses on the table. The wonderful water sparkled like diamonds. The four people again drank the water. A moment later they felt young!

"We are young! We are young!" they cried with joy.

They were like happy youngsters who were **having a good time**. They laughed and shouted and ran wildly around the room.

The Widow Wycherly rushed up to the doctor's chair. There was a smile on her rosy face.

"Doctor, you dear old man," she said, "come dance with me."

"Please excuse me," he answered softly. "I am old and sick. I have not danced for many years." The doctor pointed to the others and said, "But any of these three young men would be happy to dance with you."

"Dance with me!" shouted Colonel Killigrew.

"No, dance with *me*!" yelled Mr. Gascon.

"Dance with *me*!" exclaimed Mr. Medbourne.

They all gathered around her. Mr. Gascon grabbed her by one

hand and Mr. Medbourne grabbed her by the other. Colonel Killigrew threw his arm around the young woman's waist.

They were young and in love! Each man pulled her to himself, shouting over and over, "Dance with *me*! Dance with *me*!"

A moment later they were shoving each other. Then they were fighting. They were grabbing fiercely at each other's throats. They wanted to kill each other.

As they struggled back and forth, the table was knocked over. The vase fell to the ground and smashed into a thousand pieces. The **precious** water from the Fountain of Youth flowed slowly across the floor.

"Gentlemen! Gentlemen!" exclaimed Dr. Heidegger. "You must stop this fighting at once."

They stopped and looked at old Dr. Heidegger. He was sitting in his chair. He was looking at the rose from fifty-five years ago.

"My poor Sylvia's rose!" said Dr. Heidegger, holding it up to the light. "It appears to be fading again."

And so it was. While his guests were looking at it, the rose began to **shrink**. Soon it was as dry and brown as when the doctor first took it out of his book.

Dr. Heidegger's guests suddenly felt cold and began to shiver. They wondered if they would also grow old again, like the doctor's rose. They looked at each other and watched as their hair turned gray.

"Are we old again?" they asked Dr. Heidegger.

"Yes, friends," said Dr. Heidegger, "you are old. And look! The water from the Fountain of Youth has spilled on the ground. Well, I am not sorry about that. No! If the fountain were here right now, I would not drink from it."

The doctor looked closely at his friends. "I see that you have learned nothing from your mistakes," he said. "That is the lesson you have taught me!"

But the doctor's friends were not listening to him. They were making plans to leave for Florida at once. There they hoped to find the Fountain of Youth. They wanted to drink from it morning, noon, and night.

A **symbol** is something that "stands for," or *represents*, something else. For example, around February 14 (Valentine's Day), you will see many red hearts. The heart is a *symbol*. It stands for love. In "Dr. Heidegger's Experiment," the rose is more than a flower. It is also a symbol. You will read more about this symbol in THINKING ABOUT LITERATURE.

Meet the Author

Nathaniel Hawthorne (1804–1864) was born in Salem, Massachusetts. He started writing short stories, and then began to write novels. *The Scarlet Letter* is Hawthorne's best-known novel. It made him famous around the world. Hawthorne is one of America's greatest writers.

CHECK YOUR READING

Put an **X** in the box next to the correct answer.

Reading Comprehension

1. Dr. Heidegger told his friends to think about
   - ☐ **a.** how happy they were.
   - ☐ **b.** the mistakes they made while they were young.
   - ☐ **c.** how sad they were.

2. After the four people drank the water, they felt
   - ☐ **a.** weaker.
   - ☐ **b.** younger.
   - ☐ **c.** sicker.

3. Colonel Killigrew told the Widow Wycherly that she was
   - ☐ **a.** old.
   - ☐ **b.** acting foolishly.
   - ☐ **c.** beautiful again.

4. The Widow Wycherly asked the doctor to
   - ☐ **a.** dance with her.
   - ☐ **b.** marry her.
   - ☐ **c.** give her some medicine.

5. At the end of the story, the rose
   - ☐ **a.** became brown and dry.
   - ☐ **b.** was destroyed during the fight.
   - ☐ **c.** became more beautiful.

6. Dr. Heidegger's friends made plans to
   - ☐ **a.** go to a restaurant.
   - ☐ **b.** find the Fountain.
   - ☐ **c.** visit him again.

Vocabulary

7. With trembling hands, they raised the glasses to their lips. The word *trembling* means
   - ☐ **a.** shaking.
   - ☐ **b.** strong.
   - ☐ **c.** large.

8. The precious water from the Fountain flowed across the floor. The word *precious* means
   - ☐ **a.** worth a lot.
   - ☐ **b.** worth very little.
   - ☐ **c.** worth nothing.

9. The rose began to shrink and grow old. The verb *to shrink* means
   - ☐ **a.** to get bigger.
   - ☐ **b.** to get smaller.
   - ☐ **c.** to get harder.

Idioms

10. They laughed loudly and had a good time. When you are *having a good time*, you are
    - ☐ **a.** looking at your watch.
    - ☐ **b.** going to a party.
    - ☐ **c.** enjoying yourself.

How many questions did you answer correctly? Circle your score. Then fill in your score on the Score Chart on page 190.

Number Correct	Score
1	10
2	20
3	30
4	40
5	50
6	60
7	70
8	80
9	90
10	100

Understanding the Story

Exercise A ~ Checking Comprehension

Answer each question by writing a complete sentence. Begin each sentence with a capital letter, and end each sentence with a period. You may use the line numbers in parentheses to help you.

1. How many glasses did Dr. Heidegger fill with water? (1)

_____

2. What did Dr. Heidegger ask his friends to think about? (5)

_____

3. After the four people drank the water, how did they feel? (15)

_____

4. What was the Widow Wycherly afraid she would see when she looked in the mirror? (32)

_____

5. What was Colonel Killigrew thinking about? (37)

_____

6. What was Mr. Medbourne figuring out? (39)

_____

7. What happened to the table when the men began to fight? (72)

_____

8. What happened to the vase? (73)

_____

9. Where did Dr. Heidegger's friends plan to go? (97)

_____

10. What did the four people want to do at the Fountain of Youth? (98)

_____

Exercise B ~ Building Sentences

Make sentences by adding the correct letter.

1. _____ Dr. Heidegger filled the glasses with	**a.**	grew dark.
2. _____ Their white hair	**b.**	waved his arms.
3. _____ The Widow Wycherly knew that the Colonel	**c.**	did not always tell the truth.
4. _____ Mr. Gascon climbed on a chair and	**d.**	her face in the mirror.
5. _____ The Widow Wycherly kept smiling at	**e.**	water from the Fountain of Youth.

Now do questions 6–10 the same way.

6. _____ They laughed and shouted and ran	**a.**	in love with her.
7. _____ The widow asked the doctor	**b.**	were fighting with each other.
8. _____ The three men were	**c.**	spilled on the ground.
9. _____ A moment later, the men	**d.**	wildly around the room.
10. _____ The water from the fountain	**e.**	to dance with her.

Now write the sentences on the lines below. Remember to begin each sentence with a capital letter and to end each sentence with a period.

1. _____

2. _____

3. _____

4. _____

5. _____

6. _____

7. _____

8. _____

9. _____

10. _____

Exercise C ~ Adding Vocabulary

In the box are 8 words from the story. Complete each sentence by adding the correct word.

sparkled	eager	fading	adjusted
imagining	struggled	selected	shrewd

1. The old people wanted to drink the water at once; they were

   _____ to drink.

2. The doctor was glad that he had _____ his four friends for the experiment.

3. Colonel Killigrew was thinking about dinner; he was _____ plates piled with food.

4. Mr. Medbourne was figuring out a _____ business deal that would make him rich.

5. The wonderful water _____ like diamonds.

6. The Widow Wycherly put her hands up to her head and

   _____ her hat.

7. During the fight, the men _____ with each other.

8. The rose was losing its color; it was _____.

Exercise D ~ Using Verbs Correctly

Fill in the blanks in each sentence to form the **past continuous** tense. Use *was* or *were* plus the **present participle** (the *ing* form) of the verb in parentheses. Some examples are *was going, were crying, was* not *speaking.* The first sentence has been done for you.

1. Colonel Killigrew ___was___ ___singing___ loudly. (sing)

2. Mr. Medbourne _____ _____ his arms wildly. (wave)

3. The three men _____ _____ in a very strange way. (act)

4. The Widow Wycherly _____ _____ at her face in the mirror. (smile)

5. A moment later the men _____ _____ each other. (shove)

6. They _____ _____ at each other's throats. (grab)

7. Dr. Heidegger _____ _____ in his chair. (sit)

8. He _____ _____ at the rose from fifty-five years ago. (look)

9. The doctor's friends _____ not _____ to him. (listen)

10. They _____ _____ plans to leave for Florida at once. (make)

Write your own sentences in the **past continuous** tense by using the verbs in parentheses.

11. (was filling) _____

_____

12. (were talking) _____

_____

13. (were drinking) _____

_____

14. (was shouting) _____

_____

15. (were hoping) _____

_____

Exercise E ~ Putting Words in Order

Unscramble each sentence by putting the words in the correct order. Write each sentence on the line. Each sentence is in the **past tense**.

1. a / very / had / water / sweet smell / The

_____.

2. filled / Dr. Heidegger / glasses / their / top / to the

_____.

3. people / the / four / water / The / drank

_____.

4. ran / wildly / They / room / the / around

_____.

5. to / She / up / chair / doctor's / rushed / the

_____.

6. thousand / It / into / broke / pieces / a

_____.

7. mistakes / their / from / nothing / learned / They

_____.

8. Florida / plans / made / leave / They / to / for

_____.

Exercise F ~ Vocabulary Review

Write a complete sentence for each word or group of words.

1. liquid _____

_____

2. fortune _____

_____

3. astonished _____

_____

4. conceited _____

_____

5. dishonest _____

_____

6. count on _____

_____

7. eager _____

_____

8. sparkled _____

_____

9. struggled _____

_____

10. precious _____

_____

STUDYING THE STORY

A. Looking Back at the Story

Discuss these questions with your partner or with the group. Your teacher may ask you to write your answer to one of the questions.

- Mr. Medbourne, Mr. Gascon, Colonel Killigrew, and the Widow Wycherly all were very unhappy people. Tell why.

- At the end of the story, Dr. Heidegger said, "If the fountain were here right now, I would not drink from it." Why wouldn't Dr. Heidegger drink from the Fountain of Youth?

- Suppose that Dr. Heidegger's friends found the Fountain of Youth. Do you think that it would bring them happiness? Explain your answer.

- Dr. Heidegger's friends were eager to be young. If you could be any age you wanted to be, what age would you choose? (Perhaps you want to be the age you are now.) Give reasons for your answer.

B. Charting Character Traits

A character in a story may be brave, friendly, or wise. These are **character traits** that describe, or tell about, the character. Fill in the chart below by writing in one important *character trait* for each character listed. Then write a sentence that supports, or gives information about, the trait you chose. One character trait is already listed.

Character	Trait	Supporting Information
Mr. Medbourne	*greedy*	
Mr. Gascon		
Colonel Killigrew		
The Widow Wycherly		

THINKING ABOUT LITERATURE

1. In literature, a **symbol** is something that "stands for," or *represents*, something else. For example, a sudden, terrible *storm* may stand for, or be a sign, that something bad is going to happen. But if the *sun* breaks through the dark clouds, that is probably a sign that things will get better.

   In "Dr. Heidegger's Experiment," the **rose** is a symbol. At the beginning of the story, the rose was fifty-five years old and was dried-out and faded. When Dr. Heidegger poured water from the Fountain of Youth on to the rose, it bloomed and became fresh. But the rose soon began to fade, and it became as dry and old as it was before. Who might the rose "stand for," or represent, in the story? Be sure to use the word *symbol* in your answer.

   _____

   _____

   _____

2. Were you able to find the **theme**, or the main idea, of "Dr. Heidegger's Experiment"? You were right if you said the theme is that people do not learn from their mistakes.

   At the end of the story, Dr. Heidegger told his friends, "I see that you have learned nothing from your mistakes." On the lines below, explain why Dr. Heidegger said that his friends had not learned from their mistakes.

   _____

   _____

   _____

   _____

   _____

   _____

   _____

SIX ROWS OF FLOWERS

BY TOSHIO MORI

GETTING READY TO READ

1. The Story and You

In "Six Rows of Flowers," you will meet Uncle Hiroshi and little Tatsuo. Uncle Hiroshi decides to teach Tatsuo some lessons about life. Can you remember a time when someone tried to teach *you* something—or a time when you tried to teach someone else? Tell what happened.

2. Learning About Literature

Toshio Mori is the author of "Six Rows of Flowers." This story, like most of Mori's Stories, is about his experiences as a Japanese American. When an author writes a book about his or her life, the book is called an **autobiography**. "Six Rows of Flowers" tells about things that happened in Mori's life. Therefore, it is an *autobiographical* story.

3. Looking Ahead

Think about the title of this story. Then look at the picture on the left. How do you think the people in the story earn money? What do you think the man might be telling the boy? Read on to see if you are right.

SIX ROWS OF FLOWERS

BY TOSHIO MORI

PART 1

Our family lived and worked at a nursery. Growing and selling flowers was the way we earned our living.

When our little nephew Tatsuo was seven years old, he came to live at the nursery. He watched everything the adults there did. After school and on weekends, he went out into our fields. While we worked, he asked us many questions.

Little Tatsuo asked, "How did the plants get here? What is water? What are the bugs and what do they do? Why do birds sing?" and so on.

I said to Uncle Hiroshi, "We must do something about this. We can't spend our time continually answering little Tatsuo's questions. And some of the questions are hard to answer. We don't want to give him wrong information. We must do something."

"I agree," said Uncle Hiroshi. "We'll let little Tatsuo learn through experience. Experience is a good teacher."

So Uncle Hiroshi took little Tatsuo and brought him out into the fields. He showed him the many rows of plants that were growing there. We mostly grew pompons, small plants that have beautiful flowers.

"Do you know what these are?" said Uncle Hiroshi. He pointed to the pompons.

"Yes," said little Tatsuo. "Plants. They are **valuable**."

"You know that later these plants will have flowers. We sell the flowers to get money for food."

Nephew Tatsuo nodded. "Yes," he said. "I knew that."

"All right," Uncle Hiroshi said. "I am going to give you six rows of pompons. They are yours. You own them now. Take care of them. You must make them grow and have beautiful flowers."

Little Tatsuo looked proud and happy.

"Do you really want to do that?" Uncle Hiroshi asked.

"Sure!" Tatsuo said.

"You can begin right away," Uncle Hiroshi said. "But first, let me tell you something. You cannot quit once you start. These six rows of flowers are yours. You must not let them die. You must make them grow and have flowers."

"Okay," little Tatsuo said. "I will."

"There is a lot of work to do," said Uncle Hiroshi. "Every day you must take care of your plants. School is closed now for the summer. But you'll have **to take care of** the plants even after school opens. You'll have to take care of the plants, rain or shine."

"All right," Tatsuo said. "I'll do it. You'll see."

So little Tatsuo began to work on his six rows of pompons, and we were able to do our work without being bothered by him.

Every once in a while, however, little Tatsuo would run excitedly to Uncle Hiroshi.

"Uncle Hiroshi, come with me!" he said. "There are bugs on my plants. They're big bugs—green bugs with black dots. What should I do?"

"They're bad bugs," Uncle Hiroshi said. "You must spray them."

"But I don't have any spray."

"All right. I will spray them for you today," Uncle Hiroshi said. "Tomorrow I will get you some spray. Then you must spray your own plants."

As Uncle Hiroshi sprayed the plants, he noticed that there were
some tall weeds[1] among the pompons. He also saw that young weeds
were beginning to grow in all of the six rows.

"Those weeds attract the bugs," Uncle Hiroshi said. "Pull out the
weeds. Keep the place clean."

It took Tatsuo several days to pull out the weeds. And since he
didn't pull all of them up by their roots, a few weeks later the weeds
came back. Sometimes, Uncle Hiroshi came around to check the
moisture in the soil. He put his hand on the earth and said,
"Tatsuo, your plants need water. They need water *now* during the hot
summer. If you wait, it will be too late."

Tatsuo took a hose and began to water the plants.

"Water the plants evenly," advised Uncle Hiroshi. "Don't hold the
hose in one place for a long time and in another place for a short
time. And put lots of water on the leaves."

Nephew Tatsuo worked at the job through the summer and on
into the fall, although at times he didn't seem very interested.
Whenever Tatsuo lost interest, Uncle Hiroshi looked at the six rows
of flowers and seemed very pleased.

"This is wonderful!" he said with enthusiasm. "Your pompons are
growing very fast. Soon they'll have flowers."

"Do you think so?" Nephew Tatsuo asked.

"Sure. You will have lots of flowers. When you have enough to
make a big **bunch**, I'll sell them for you at the flower market."

"Really?" Nephew Tatsuo said. "At the flower market?"

Uncle Hiroshi laughed. "Of course. That's the place where people
buy flowers, isn't it?"

---

1. *weeds*: plants that grow very quickly and kill other plants

CHECK YOUR READING

Put an **X** in the box next to the correct answer.

Reading Comprehension

1. How old was little Tatsuo when he came to live at the nursery?
- [ ] **a.** six years old
- [ ] **b.** seven years old
- [ ] **c.** ten years old

2. After school little Tatsuo
- [ ] **a.** stayed in his room.
- [ ] **b.** played with his friends.
- [ ] **c.** went into the fields and asked questions.

3. Uncle Hiroshi gave Tatsuo
- [ ] **a.** a beautiful flower.
- [ ] **b.** two or three plants.
- [ ] **c.** six rows of pompons.

4. Uncle Hiroshi said that it was important to
- [ ] **a.** let the weeds grow.
- [ ] **b.** give the plants water.
- [ ] **c.** make sure the plants didn't get wet.

5. Little Tatsuo
- [ ] **a.** wasn't always interested in his work.
- [ ] **b.** always worked hard.
- [ ] **c.** never asked for help.

6. Uncle Hiroshi said that he would
- [ ] **a.** give Tatsuo money for working at the nursery.
- [ ] **a.** do Tatsuo's work.
- [ ] **a.** sell Tatsuo's flowers.

Vocabulary

7. The plants were valuable. They were sold to get money for food. The word *valuable* means
- [ ] **a.** worth a lot.
- [ ] **b.** very tall.
- [ ] **c.** very short.

8. Little Tatsuo needed enough flowers to make a big bunch. The word *bunch* means
- [ ] **a.** money.
- [ ] **b.** market.
- [ ] **c.** group.

9. Uncle Hiroshi checked the moisture to see if the plants needed water. The word *moisture* means
- [ ] **a.** how warm something is.
- [ ] **b.** how wet something is.
- [ ] **c.** how large something is.

Idioms

10. He had to take care of his plants. The idiom *to take care of* means
- [ ] **a.** to take away.
- [ ] **b.** to watch and care for.
- [ ] **c.** to stay away from.

How many questions did you answer correctly? Circle your score. Then fill in your score on the Score Chart on page 190.

Number Correct	Score
1	10
2	20
3	30
4	40
5	50
6	60
7	70
8	80
9	90
10	100

UNDERSTANDING THE STORY

Exercise A ~ Checking Comprehension

Answer each question by writing a complete sentence. Begin each sentence with a capital letter, and end each sentence with a period. You may use the line numbers in parentheses to help you.

1. Where did the family live and work? (1)

   _____

2. How old was little Tatsuo when he came to live at the nursery? (3)

   _____

3. When did Tatsuo go out into the fields? (5)

   _____

4. What are pompons? (18)

   _____

5. What did Uncle Hiroshi give Tatsuo? (26)

   _____

6. What did Tatsuo have to do every day? (37)

   _____

7. How long did it take Tatsuo to pull out the weeds? (59)

   _____

8. Why did the weeds grow back? (60)

   _____

9. How much water did the leaves need? (68)

   _____

10. Where was Uncle Hiroshi going to sell the flowers? (77)

   _____

Exercise B ~ Building Sentences

Make sentences by adding the correct letter.

1. _____ The family earned money by	**a.** were hard to answer.
2. _____ Little Tatsuo wanted to know	**b.** why the birds sing.
3. _____ Some of Tatsuo's questions	**c.** little Tatsuo to do.
4. _____ Uncle Hiroshi warned Tatsuo not to	**d.** selling flowers.
5. _____ There was a lot of work for	**e.** let the plants die.

Now do questions 6–10 the same way.

6. _____ Tatsuo said there were some	**a.** among Tatsuo's plants.
7. _____ Weeds were growing	**b.** the summer and the fall.
8. _____ Uncle Hiroshi told Tatsuo to	**c.** were growing fast.
9. _____ Tatsuo worked there in	**d.** keep the place clean.
10. _____ Tatsuo's plants	**e.** bugs on his plants.

Now write the sentences on the lines below. Remember to begin each sentence with a capital letter and to end each sentence with a period.

1. _____

2. _____

3. _____

4. _____

5. _____

6. _____

7. _____

8. _____

9. _____

10. _____

Exercise C ~ Adding Vocabulary

In the box are 8 words from the story. Complete each sentence by adding the correct word.

hose	adults	information	enthusiasm
experience	roots	spray	attract

1. Little Tatsuo watched everything the _____ did at the nursery.

2. The adults didn't want to give little Tatsuo _____ that was wrong.

3. They let Tatsuo work at the nursery so that he could learn through

   _____ .

4. Uncle Hiroshi told little Tatsuo to pull out the weeds because weeds

   _____ bugs.

5. To kill the bugs, Uncle Hiroshi had to _____ them.

6. Since little Tatsuo didn't pull out the weeds by their _____ , the weeds grew back later.

7. Tatsuo took a _____ and began to water the plants.

8. "This is wonderful!" Uncle Hiroshi said with _____ .

Exercise D ~ Using Verbs Correctly

Fill in the blanks in each sentence by writing the **future tense** of the verb in parentheses. Use *will* plus the verb. The first one has been done for you.

1. Later in the season, the plants ___*will*___ ___*have*___ flowers. (have)

2. Uncle Hiroshi told little Tatsuo, "Tomorrow I _____ _____ you six rows of pompons." (give)

3. Little Tatsuo said, "I _____ _____ the plants and help them grow." (watch)

4. Tatsuo's plants _____ _____ a lot of water. (need)

5. If you don't give plants enough water, they _____ _____ . (die)

6. Uncle Hiroshi said, "Later, I _____ _____ you some spray for the bugs." (get)

7. If you do not pull out the weeds by their roots, the weeds _____ _____ back. (grow)

8. Uncle Hiroshi thought, "We _____ _____ little Tatsuo how to grow flowers." (teach)

9. Next week Uncle Hiroshi _____ _____ to the flower market. (go)

10. When little Tatsuo has enough flowers, Uncle Hiroshi _____ _____ them. (sell)

Write your own sentences in the **future tense** by using the verbs in parentheses.

11. (will work) _____

_____

12. (will try) _____

_____

Exercise E ~ Picking a Pronoun

Fill in each blank by adding the correct **possessive pronoun**. Use each pronoun once.

my	our	its
his	yours	theirs

1. We worked at a nursery. Selling flowers was the way we earned

    _____ living.

2. Uncle Hiroshi told little Tatsuo, "Here are six rows of pompons. Now they

    are _____."

3. Tatsuo's flowers were dry. Tatsuo took a hose and began to water

    _____ plants.

4. Little Tatsuo said to Uncle Hiroshi, "Tell me what to do. There are bugs

    on _____ plants."

5. The family owned the nursery. It was _____.

6. Uncle Hiroshi dug up some plants with a shovel. He held the shovel by

    _____ handle.

Write your own sentences by using the possessive pronouns in parentheses.

7. (mine) _____

    _____

8. (ours) _____

    _____

9. (yours) _____

    _____

10. (their) _____

    _____

Before You Read Part 2

In Part 1, Uncle Hiroshi lets Tatsuo take care of six rows of flowers. Tatsuo is proud and happy, but he is not a good gardener. Do you think that Tatsuo's flowers will grow? See if you are right.

PART 2

One day Tatsuo came by with a tennis ball. He wanted us to play catch with him. It was the busiest time of the year at the nursery. We were so busy that we even worked on Sundays.

"Nephew Tatsuo," said Uncle Hiroshi, "don't you know we all
5   have **responsibilities**? Uncle Hiroshi has a lot of work to do today. Now is the busiest time of the year. You also have a lot of work to do. You should be busy now. Do you know whether your pompons are wet or dry?"

"No, Uncle Hiroshi," he said. "I don't remember."

10   "Then take care of it right away," Uncle Hiroshi said.

Nephew Tatsuo ran over to the six rows of flowers. He came running back. "Uncle Hiroshi, they're still wet," he said.

"All right," Uncle Hiroshi said. "But did you see those holes in the ground with little mounds of earth near them?"

15   "Yes. They're gopher holes," little Tatsuo said.

"Right," Uncle Hiroshi said. "Did you catch the gopher?"

"No," said Tatsuo.

"Then take care of it. Take care of it right away," Uncle Hiroshi said.

Nephew Tatsuo ran off to take care of it.

20   One day late in October, Uncle Hiroshi's pompons started to bloom. Uncle Hiroshi cut the flowers and put them into bunches to take to the market. By this time, Tatsuo was eager to see *his* pompons bloom. But by now Nephew Tatsuo's six rows of flowers looked like a piece of earth covered with tall weeds. Not many
25   pompons grew higher than the weeds.

A few of the plants in the six rows of flowers **survived**. But most of the plants had died before the cool weather arrived. Some died because the earth was too dry. Some were killed by the gopher. And some were crushed by the tall weeds that were growing everywhere.

30   When the other pompons at the nursery began to bloom, everyone became worried.

"We must do something about Tatsuo's six rows of flowers," Tatsuo's father said. "His six rows of flowers are worthless, and the bugs on them are coming over to our flowers. Let's cut down his

rows and burn them."

"No," said Uncle Hiroshi. "We cannot do that. That is **out of the question**. That would hurt little Tatsuo very much. Let his plants stay."

So little Tatsuo's six rows of flowers stayed. The weeds, the plants, and the bugs all stayed. A little later a few of the plants began to have flowers. Nephew Tatsuo ran around looking for Uncle Hiroshi. Tatsuo called out, "The flowers are here!" He wanted to know when he could cut them.

"Today," Uncle Hiroshi said. "Cut them today, and I will sell them at the market tomorrow."

Little Tatsuo had just enough flowers to make one bunch.

The next day at the flower market, Uncle Hiroshi sold the bunch of flowers. When Uncle Hiroshi came home, Nephew Tatsuo ran to the car.

"Did you sell the bunch of flowers, Uncle Hiroshi?" Nephew Tatsuo asked.

"Sure. They were easy to sell. They were healthy, carefully grown, very good flowers."

Nephew Tatsuo ran around excitedly. First he went to his father. "Papa!" he said. "Someone bought my pompons!" Then he ran over to me and said, "My flowers were sold! Uncle Hiroshi sold my pompons!"

At noon, after lunch was over, Uncle Hiroshi gave Nephew Tatsuo the money he got for selling Tatsuo's flowers.

"What should I do with this money?" Tatsuo asked us all, his eyes shining.

Tatsuo's father said, "Put it in your toy bank."

"No," said Uncle Hiroshi. "Let him do whatever he wants with the money. Let him spend it and enjoy his money."

"Do you want to spend your money?" I asked Tatsuo.

"Yes," he said.

"Then do anything you want with it," said Uncle Hiroshi. "Buy anything you want. Go and have a good time. It is your money."

The next Sunday we did not see Nephew Tatsuo all day. When Tatsuo came back late in the afternoon, Uncle Hiroshi said, "What did you do today?"

Tatsuo said, "I went to a movie. Then I bought an ice cream cone. On my way home I watched a baseball game at the school. I bought popcorn there. I have five cents left."

Uncle Hiroshi said, "You saved something. That is good."

Uncle Hiroshi, Tatsuo's father, and I sat in the shade. It was still hot, although it was late in the day. We sat and watched Tatsuo riding around and around in the yard on his little red bicycle.

Tatsuo's father said, "Next year he will forget about what he did this year. He will be wild again next year."

"Next year is not here yet," said Uncle Hiroshi.

"Do you think he will want to grow pompons again?" Tatsuo's father asked.

"He enjoys praise," replied Uncle Hiroshi. "And he takes pride in good work well done. We will see."

"He is probably the worst gardener in the country," I said. "He is probably the worst gardener in the world."

"Probably," said Uncle Hiroshi.

That night the whole family sat at the table and ate. We talked about what kind of year it was. We talked about the flower business and the flower crop. We talked about little Tatsuo's work, about what he had done, and about what he could do in the future.

Remember, when an author writes a book about his or her life, the book is called an **autobiography**. "Six Rows of Flowers" tells about things that happened in Toshio Mori's life. Therefore, this is called an *autobiographical* story.

Meet the Author

Toshio Mori (1910–1980) grew up in California. He has written hundreds of stories. Most of them are about his experiences as a Japanese American. Mori worked for many years in a flower shop owned by his brothers. You can see how that led him to write "Six Rows of Flowers." Mori's most famous book is *Yokohama, California*, a collection of short stories.

CHECK YOUR READING

Put an **X** in the box next to the correct answer.

How many questions did you answer correctly? Circle your score. Then fill in your score on the Score Chart on page 190.

Number Correct	Score
1	10
2	20
3	30
4	40
5	50
6	60
7	70
8	80
9	90
10	100

Reading Comprehension

1. The family didn't play catch with little Tatsuo because they
   - ☐ **a.** were too busy working.
   - ☐ **b.** were angry with him.
   - ☐ **c.** didn't know how to play catch.

2. Tatsuo's six rows of flowers were
   - ☐ **a.** growing very well.
   - ☐ **b.** the best flowers in the nursery.
   - ☐ **c.** covered with tall weeds.

3. Little Tatsuo's father wanted to
   - ☐ **a.** give Tatsuo more flowers.
   - ☐ **b.** burn Tatsuo's rows.
   - ☐ **c.** let Tatsuo play all day.

4. Little Tatsuo had just enough flowers to make
   - ☐ **a.** one bunch.
   - ☐ **b.** two bunches.
   - ☐ **c.** three bunches.

5. What did little Tatsuo do with the money he got for his flowers?
   - ☐ **a.** He put it in his toy bank.
   - ☐ **b.** He gave it to his uncle.
   - ☐ **c.** He went to a movie.

6. Little Tatsuo saved
   - ☐ **a.** five cents.
   - ☐ **b.** ten cents.
   - ☐ **c.** twenty-five cents.

7. The family thought that little Tatsuo was
   - ☐ **a.** a very good gardener.
   - ☐ **b.** the best gardener in the country.
   - ☐ **c.** the worst gardener in the country.

Vocabulary

8. They could not play with little Tatsuo because they had many responsibilities. The word *responsibilities* means
   - ☐ **a.** time to have fun.
   - ☐ **b.** things you must do.
   - ☐ **c.** places to visit.

9. Most plants died, but a few survived. The word *survived* means
   - ☐ **a.** were sold.
   - ☐ **b.** were killed.
   - ☐ **c.** lived.

Idioms

10. Uncle Hiroshi said it was out of the question to burn Tatsuo's flowers. That would hurt him. The idiom *out of the question* means
    - ☐ **a.** was a good idea.
    - ☐ **b.** was something to talk about.
    - ☐ **c.** was not possible.

Understanding the Story

Exercise A ~ Checking Comprehension

Answer each question by writing a complete sentence. Begin each sentence with a capital letter, and end each sentence with a period. You may use the line numbers in parentheses to help you.

1. Why did the family work on Sundays? (3)

   _____

2. Why didn't Uncle Hiroshi play catch with little Tatsuo? (5)

   _____

3. What made holes in the ground? (15)

   _____

4. When did Uncle Hiroshi's pompons start to bloom? (20)

   _____

5. What covered Nephew Tatsuo's six rows of pompons? (24)

   _____

6. When did most of Tatsuo's plants die? (27)

   _____

7. What did Tatsuo's father want to do with little Tatsuo's rows? (34)

   _____

8. Where did Uncle Hiroshi sell Tatsuo's flowers? (46)

   _____

9. What did Tatsuo's father want little Tatsuo to do with the money? (61)

   _____

10. How much money did little Tatsuo save? (73)

    _____

Exercise B ~ Building Sentences

Make sentences by adding the correct letter.

1. _____ They were so busy they

2. _____ Uncle Hiroshi asked Tatsuo if

3. _____ Uncle Hiroshi took

4. _____ Some of Tatsuo's flowers were

5. _____ There were some bugs

a. the flowers to the market.

b. his plants were wet.

c. worked on Sundays.

d. on Tatsuo's plants.

e. crushed by the weeds.

Now do questions 6–10 the same way.

6. _____ Uncle Hiroshi did not want to

7. _____ Uncle Hiroshi said Tatsuo's flowers

8. _____ Tatsuo went to a movie and

9. _____ They watched Tatsuo ride

10. _____ That night they talked

a. about the flower business.

b. cut down Tatsuo's plants.

c. his bicycle.

d. bought an ice cream cone.

e. were easy to sell.

Now write the sentences on the lines below. Remember to begin each sentence with a capital letter and to end each sentence with a period.

1. _____

2. _____

3. _____

4. _____

5. _____

6. _____

7. _____

8. _____

9. _____

10. _____

Exercise C ~ Adding Vocabulary

In the box are 8 words from the story. Complete each sentence by adding the
correct word.

shade	future	mounds	worthless
gopher	praise	bloom	pride

1. They saw holes in the ground. Near the holes were little

   _____ of earth.

2. The holes in the ground were made by an animal. The animal was a

   _____ .

3. One day Uncle Hiroshi's plants began to have flowers. The plants were

   beginning to _____ .

4. Little Tatsuo's plants were not worth anything. They were

   _____ .

5. It was very hot in the sun. Therefore, they sat in the _____ .

6. Uncle Hiroshi told Tatsuo that his flowers were very good. Little Tatsuo

   enjoyed the _____ .

7. Little Tatsuo liked his plants very much. He took _____ in
   them.

8. The family talked about what little Tatsuo had already done. Then they

   talked about what he could do in the _____ .

Exercise D ~ Using Verbs Correctly

Fill in each blank using the **past tense** of the irregular verb in parentheses.

1. After a while, the weeds _____ higher than the flowers. (grow)

2. When the bugs covered Tatsuo's plants, everyone _____ worried. (become)

3. Some of the plants _____ to have flowers. (begin)

4. The gopher _____ holes in the ground. (make)

5. Little Tatsuo never _____ the gopher. (catch)

6. Uncle Hiroshi _____ a lot of work at the nursery. (do)

7. Little Tatsuo cut some of his flowers and _____ them to Uncle Hiroshi. (bring)

8. Uncle Hiroshi _____ little Tatsuo's plants at the flower market. (sell)

9. Uncle Hiroshi _____ some money for little Tatsuo's flowers. (get)

10. Tatsuo was happy when he _____ that Uncle Hiroshi had sold his flowers. (hear)

11. The boy _____ most of the money that his uncle gave him. (spend)

12. Little Tatsuo watched a baseball game and _____ an ice cream cone. (buy)

13. Tatsuo _____ around and around on his bicycle. (ride)

14. At night the family sat at the table and _____ dinner. (eat)

15. The family often _____ about little Tatsuo and the flower business. (speak)

Exercise E ~ Adding Punctuation

The following passage needs punctuation marks. Add capital letters, periods, question marks, a comma, and quotation marks. Then write the corrected passage on the lines below.

uncle hiroshi went to the flower market in the morning he came back later that day little tatsuo ran to the car tatsuo was very excited his voice was shaking he asked did you sell my flowers did you get some money for them

_____

_____

_____

_____

_____

_____

_____

_____

_____

Exercise F ~ Vocabulary Review

Write a complete sentence for each word or group of words.

1. adults _____

_____

2. enthusiam _____

_____

3. valuable _____

_____

4. moisture _____

_____

5. to take care of _____

_____

6. praise _____

_____

7. pride _____

_____

8. responsibility _____

_____

9. survived _____

_____

10. out of the question _____

_____

STUDYING THE STORY

A. Looking Back at the Story

Discuss these questions with your partner or with the group. Your teacher may ask you to write your answer to one of the questions.

- Why did Uncle Hiroshi give little Tatsuo six rows of flowers? Do you think that Uncle Hiroshi should have given Tatsuo the flowers? Explain.

- Tell all the jobs that Tatsuo had to do to keep his flowers from dying.

- Tatsuo's father wanted Tatsuo to save the money he earned. Uncle Hiroshi said, "Let him do whatever he wants with the money." Who do you think was right? Explain.

- Do you think that little Tatsuo will work at the nursery again next year? Why?

B. Charting Lessons from the Story

"Six Rows of Flowers" is a story that teaches many lessons. There are lessons about work, responsibility, and ways of learning. There are lessons about family and being kind. Think carefully about the story. Then, on the chart below, list some of the lessons the story teaches. List at least one lesson in each column.

Lessons about work and responsibility	Lessons about ways of learning	Lessons about family and being kind

THINKING ABOUT LITERATURE

1. The **narrator** is the person who tells the story. In "Six Rows of Flowers," Toshio Mori is the *narrator*. The story is *autobiographical* because Mori tells about people he knows and events from his life.

   Suppose a narrator writes a book that tells the story of his or her life. What is this kind of book called?

   _____

2. Little Tatsuo was proud of his flowers. When Tatsuo got money for them, he was *very* proud. Now it's time for *you* to be a narrator and to write something that is **autobiographical**.

   Write about a time when *you* felt proud. It might be a time when you helped a friend or someone in your family. It might be a time when you won a prize, built something, acted in a play, or did well in a sport. It might be a time when you worked hard enough to do better in a class at school. Perhaps something else made you proud. Be sure to tell:

   ■ what you did

   ■ where and when it happened

   ■ why it made you feel proud

   _____

   _____

   _____

   _____

   _____

   _____

   _____

   _____

   _____

   _____

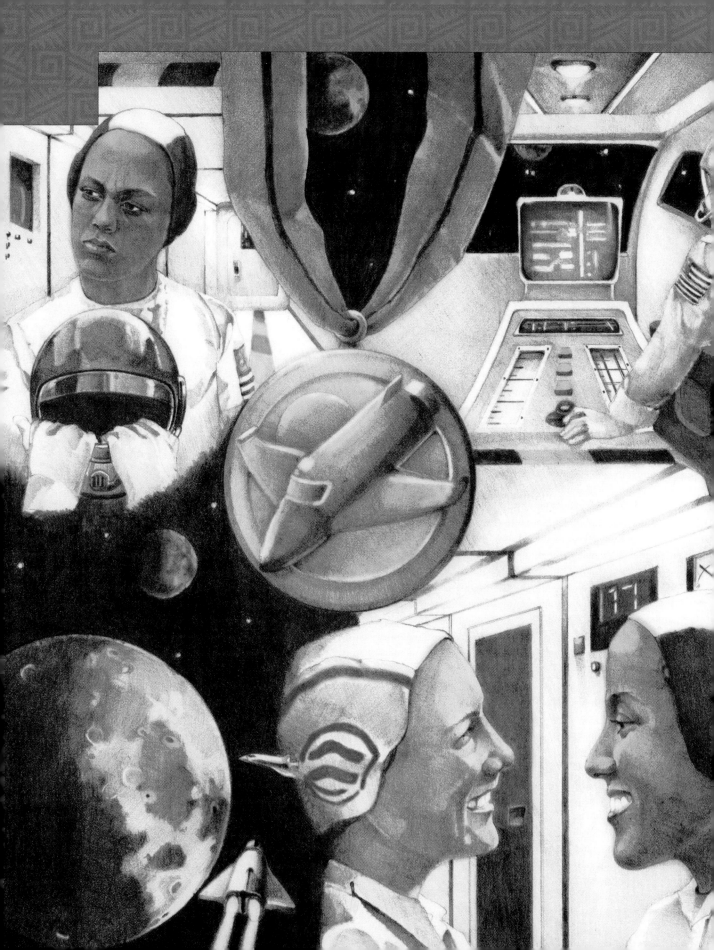

Space Star

By Lael J. Littke

Getting Ready to Read

1. The Story and You

In "Space Star," you will meet Narda and Rel. They are people who do not live on Earth. Narda and Rel live on places far away in space. Do you think there are people who live on another planet somewhere? Tell why.

2. Learning About Literature

"Space Star" is a **science fiction** story. Science fiction stories often take place in strange worlds that are very different from our own. In those worlds, there may be unusual creatures that are able to do amazing things. The stories often take place in the future, hundreds or thousands of years from now. The word fiction means "not true." Can you see how *science fiction* got its name?

3. Looking Ahead

Look at the picture on the left. Describe the people you see. Who do you think those people are? Do you think the story takes place in the past, the future, or now? Why? Read on to see if you are right.

Space Star

By Lael J. Littke

PART 1

Maris was ready, all dressed in her space suit except for the helmet. Before she put that on, she took one last look in the mirror.

"The next time I look at you," she promised, "I'll be wearing the Space Star medal. I'll be very proud of myself."

Yes, she was going to win the space race today. She was the best minicraft[1] pilot in the Galaxy Space Race.

Or was she?

Maris looked at her reflection in the mirror and thought about herself. She had worked very hard learning how to fly the small one-person minicraft. She knew she was good at it. She thought she was good enough to win the Space Star medal.

Maris put on her helmet. Then she stepped out into the corridor that led to the launching platform. Two other pilots, Narda and Rel, were also walking toward the platform. Maris knew Narda. She was a young, green-skinned woman from the fifth moon of Jupiter. Rel was a pilot from the asteroid Pallas.

Narda smiled confidently. "This is the big day, isn't it?" she asked through her helmet. It quickly translated all the languages in the galaxy.

Maris suddenly felt her own confidence fading[2]. There were **quite a few** pilots in the race, but Narda was the one who worried Maris the most. Narda flew fast and without any fear—and she wanted to win very much. She and Maris had the same scores when they tried out earlier. They had the highest scores of all the pilots. But Maris noticed that Narda didn't always fly exactly on course. She

1. *minicraft:* a small space plane

2. *fading:* growing less, disappearing

sometimes went off the route. And accuracy was as important as speed in the race.

Rel said to Maris and Narda, "This will probably be a big day for one of you. I just hope that I don't embarrass myself."

"Embarrass yourself?" said Maris. "What do you mean by that, Rel?"

Rel said, "I can't really compete with you two. I'm just a beginner. The truth is I'm not a very good pilot."

"That's not so," Maris said. "You wouldn't be here if you weren't the best minicraft pilot on Pallas."

Rel smiled. "Thanks, Maris," he said. "Anyway, I'll do my best."

They had arrived at the door that led to the launching platform. Moments later the contestants were in their minicrafts.

As soon as she was inside her small spaceship, Maris checked the control panel. Then she turned on the radio and tested it. "This is Number 34, Maris, representing Earth," she reported to the control tower.

Maris looked out the window of the minicraft and waved at the **spectators** far across the field. She knew, of course, that they couldn't see her. But it made her feel good to know that her parents, brother, and friends from Earth were in the crowd. She smiled when she thought about how proud they would be when she won the medal.

But first she had to win it!

It was time for the launching. One by one the minicrafts were moved to their places on the launching platform. Then they were sent off into space. Winning did not depend on who arrived back at the base first. It depended on who took the least time from departure[3] to return. Of course, you had to stay on the route. And you were not supposed to talk to the other pilots.

Maris saw Number 32, Rel, **soar** off into space. Number 33, Narda, was just in front of Maris. A few minutes later, Narda's minicraft took off. Then it was Maris's turn.

---

3. *departure:* leaving

CHECK YOUR READING

Put an **X** in the box next to the correct answer.

How many questions did you answer correctly? Circle your score. Then fill in your score on the Score Chart on page 190.

Number Correct	Score
1	10
2	20
3	30
4	40
5	50
6	60
7	70
8	80
9	90
10	100

Reading Comprehension

1. Maris was dressed in
- ☐ **a.** old clothing.
- ☐ **b.** her best clothes.
- ☐ **c.** a space suit.

2. Maris wanted to win
- ☐ **a.** a lot of money.
- ☐ **b.** the Space Star medal.
- ☐ **c.** a new spaceship.

3. Where did Narda come from?
- ☐ **a.** the fifth moon of Jupiter
- ☐ **b.** Earth
- ☐ **c.** the asteroid Pallas

4. Rel said that he
- ☐ **a.** was a very good pilot.
- ☐ **b.** was not a very good pilot.
- ☐ **c.** would win the race.

5. In the crowd, Maris saw
- ☐ **a.** her aunt and uncle.
- ☐ **b.** her two sisters.
- ☐ **c.** her parents, brother, and friends.

6. During the race, the pilots were not supposed to
- ☐ **a.** fly very fast.
- ☐ **b.** talk to the other pilots.
- ☐ **c.** turn on the radio.

7. What was Maris's number in the race?
- ☐ **a.** Number 32
- ☐ **b.** Number 33
- ☐ **c.** Number 34

Vocabulary

8. Maris looked out the window of her spaceship and saw spectators across the field. A *spectator* is a person who
- ☐ **a.** watches something.
- ☐ **b.** builds something.
- ☐ **c.** breaks something.

9. Maris saw Rel soar off into space. The word *soar* means
- ☐ **a.** fly up.
- ☐ **b.** fall down.
- ☐ **c.** shout loudly.

Idioms

10. There were quite a few pilots in the race. The idiom *quite a few* means
- ☐ **a.** one.
- ☐ **b.** two or three.
- ☐ **c.** many.

UNDERSTANDING THE STORY

Exercise A ~ Checking Comprehension

Answer each question by writing a complete sentence. Begin each sentence with a capital letter, and end each sentence with a period. You may use the line numbers in parentheses to help you.

1. What was Maris wearing? (1)

_____

2. What did Maris want to win? (6)

_____

3. Who did Maris meet as she walked toward the platform? (14)

_____

4. Where did Narda come from? (16)

_____

5. Who was Rel? (16)

_____

6. Which pilot worried Maris the most? (21)

_____

7. What did Maris notice about the way that Narda flew? (25)

_____

8. What did Maris do as soon as she got into her spaceship? (38)

_____

9. What did winning the race depend on? (50)

_____

10. Which pilot was just in front of Maris? (54)

_____

Exercise B ~ Building Sentences

Make sentences by adding the correct letter.

1. _____ Maris learned how to fly   **a.** win the medal.

2. _____ Maris thought she could   **b.** of all the pilots.

3. _____ Narda flew fast and wanted   **c.** best pilot on Pallas.

4. _____ Maris and Narda had the highest scores   **d.** to win very much.

5. _____ Maris thought Rel was the   **e.** a spaceship.

Now do questions 6–10 the same way.

6. _____ After Maris got into the spaceship, she   **a.** winning the medal.

7. _____ Maris waved to   **b.** Maris's turn to go.

8. _____ Maris smiled when she thought about   **c.** her parents and friends.

9. _____ One by one the minicrafts went   **d.** turned on the radio.

10. _____ A few minutes later, it was   **e.** off into space.

Now write the sentences on the lines below. Remember to begin each sentence with a capital letter and to end each sentence with a period.

1. _____

2. _____

3. _____

4. _____

5. _____

6. _____

7. _____

8. _____

9. _____

10. _____

Exercise C ~ Adding Vocabulary

In the box are 8 words from the story. Complete each sentence by adding the correct word.

contestant	reflection	confidence	compete
corridor	accuracy	translated	embarrass

1. Maris looked in the mirror. She saw her _____ there.

2. Narda believed that she was going to win the race. She had a lot of

   _____ in herself.

3. There were many pilots in the race. However, Narda was the

   _____ who worried Maris the most.

4. Rel was just a beginning pilot. He didn't think that he could

   _____ with Maris and Narda.

5. Maris put on her helmet. Then she stepped out into the

   _____ and walked to her spaceship.

6. Rel hoped that he would do well in the race. He didn't want to

   _____ himself.

7. The pilots followed the route very carefully. They knew that

   _____ was as important as speed.

8. Maris could understand what Narda was saying. That was because

   Maris's helmet _____ all the languages in the galaxy.

Exercise D ～ Using Verbs Correctly

Fill in the blanks in each sentence to form the **present perfect tense**. Use *has* or *have* plus the **past participle** of the verb in parentheses. Some examples are *has gone* and *have* not *tried*. The first sentence has been done for you.

1. Maris ___*has*___ ___*been*___ a pilot for many years. (be)

2. She _____ _____ to school to learn how to fly. (go)

3. She _____ _____ very hard. (work)

4. Narda and Rel _____ also _____ to flying school. (go)

5. However, Rel _____ not _____ for as many years. (study)

6. He _____ not _____ his classes yet. (finish)

7. Still, Rel _____ _____ a lot about flying spaceships. (learn)

8. Narda and Maris _____ _____ in space races before. (be)

9. Rel _____ never _____ in a space race before. (be)

10. Maris and Narda _____ always _____ their best to win. (try)

Write your own sentences in the **present perfect tense** by using the verbs in parentheses.

11. (has lost) _____

_____

12. (has sent) _____

_____

13. (have built) _____

_____

14. (has bought) _____

_____

Exercise E ~ Combining Sentences

Combine the two sentences into one. Write the new sentence on the line.
The first one has been done for you.

1. Maris was walking toward the platform. Narda was walking toward the platform.

   Maris and Narda were walking toward the
   platform.

2. Narda was a green-skinned woman. She was from Jupiter.

   _____

3. Rel was a pilot. He was from Pallas.

   _____

4. Rel spoke to Maris. Rel also spoke to Narda.

   _____

5. Rel got into his spaceship. Narda got into her spaceship.

   _____

6. Maris was confident. Narda was confident too.

   _____

7. Maris checked the control panel. She turned on the radio.

   _____

   _____

8. Maris looked out the window. She waved to the people.

   _____

   _____

9. Her parents were in the crowd. Her brother was in the crowd too.

   _____

   _____

10. Narda flew into space. Rel flew into space.

    _____

Before You Read Part 2

Maris thought that she was good enough to win the Galaxy Space Race. But Narda was very good, too. She flew fast, and she flew without fear. Rel was just a beginner, but he tried very hard. There were other good pilots in the race, too. Do you think that Maris will win the race? See if you are right.

PART 2

Maris's minicraft left the launching platform smoothly. Soon she was flying swiftly[1] through space, following the route. Maris saw Narda ahead of her. Narda was making a turn. She was flying very carefully today. That would make her harder to beat.

5 Maris wondered how the other contestants were doing. But she really didn't have time to worry about them. She had to look at her charts to make sure she was following the route.

During the next two hours, Maris flew around two small moons. She thought that she did everything correctly. But then she saw

10 Narda ahead of her flying very fast. Maris knew she would have to **pick up speed** and pass Narda if she wanted to win.

Maris's chance came an hour later. Narda made a very wide turn and went off course. As Narda repeated the turn, Maris flew past her.

Maris felt confident as she headed toward the final part of the

15 race. She thought to herself, "If I can keep doing everything perfectly, I'll win the medal."

Narda was nowhere in sight as Maris approached the most difficult part of the course. The pilots had to fly around a moving asteroid[2] that kept going up and down in space. They had to make sure that their ship

20 didn't get too close to the asteroid. If the ship got too close, it would get caught in the asteroid's gravity and would be pulled into the asteroid.

Maris was halfway around the asteroid when she saw another minicraft ahead of her. Maris was ready to pass the spaceship, when she realized that it was in trouble. For some reason it was losing

25 speed. If it went any slower, it would be pulled into the asteroid!

Maris lost precious seconds, but she guided her own ship close enough to see the number on the minicraft that was in trouble. It was Number 32, Rel from Pallas!

Maris pushed a button that turned on the radio. "Rel!" she

30 shouted into the microphone, "What's wrong?" Maris knew that she

---

1. *swiftly:* fast, quickly

2. *asteroid:* one of the many small planets in space

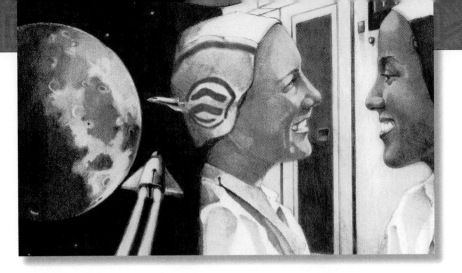

would lose points for **communicating** with another contestant. But what could she do?

"Maris! I'm glad you're near. I'm having a problem with the engine, and it's slowed my speed. I can't seem to get away from this asteroid's gravity pull. I may have to land on the asteroid."

Maris thought to herself, "He will crash! There's nowhere to land. The asteroid is covered with sharp mountain peaks!"

"No," said Maris, as calmly as she could. "You *must* stay away from the asteroid! You can keep your minicraft away from it by making the right calculations."

Rel said nervously, "I'm not sure I can do all that figuring."

"Yes, you can," Maris said firmly. "Now look at your charts and instruments."

There was silence for a moment, and then Rel spoke again. "I've tried to radio for help," he said, "but we can't get through to the base from here. We're in a dead space behind the asteroid. Will you send a rescue ship for me as soon as you get to the base?"

"Yes," Maris thought, "I could do that. I could go on and win the race, and then send back help." She could still win the Space Star medal. She wanted very much to continue. But she couldn't. Not yet anyway.

"I'll stay here with you for a while," she told Rel. "I'll contact someone else to send the rescue ship."

Just then Narda's minicraft came into view. "Narda!" Maris called over the radio. "There's no need to answer me and lose points. But send for the rescue ship as soon as you can radio the base." Maris quickly explained the problem.

Narda gave no sign that she heard the message. She just flew on.

For the first time Maris felt panic. "What if Narda didn't hear the message?" she wondered. "What if Rel and I both crash on the asteroid? We might never be found!"

Maris tried not to think about that. Rel's minicraft was losing power. It was moving slowly toward the asteroid. Maris didn't have time to think about herself. She had to help Rel do the calculations to keep from crashing. She tried not to show fear as she gave Rel instructions.

The two minicrafts were very close to the asteroid. Maris was studying it, looking for a place to land if necessary. Then she saw another spaceship approaching.

Number 33! Narda had come back!

"Narda!" Maris exclaimed. "I thought you'd be wearing the Space Star medal by now."

"I thought about it," said Narda. "But you're so far off course, I realized that I'd better **hang around** up here where the radio waves can get through. Otherwise the rescue ship will never find you."

Before Maris could say another word, Narda flew away from the asteroid. She sailed off into the distance, where she waited to guide the rescue ship to Rel.

A short time later, the rescue ship arrived. It used its powerful magnets to pull Rel's minicraft away from the asteroid. As they headed back to the base, they heard on their radios that Melona from the planet Mercury had won the race.

"I'm sorry," said Rel, after they landed safely. "I made both of you lose your chance for the medal."

But at that moment the medal didn't seem that important to Maris. She thought about the promise she made to her mirror that morning. Well, she would still keep that promise. After all, you don't have to wear a medal to be proud of yourself.

Notice that "Space Star" is a **science fiction** story. It takes place in a world that is very different from our own, and it takes place in the future, many years from now.

Meet the Author

Lael J. Littke was born in Idaho in 1929. She had several jobs before she became a full-time writer. Littke has written many books and short stories for young people. She lives in California where she writes and also teaches classes in writing.

CHECK YOUR READING

Put an **X** in the box next to the correct answer.

Reading Comprehension

1. Narda would be hard to beat because she was flying very
   - ☐ **a.** wildly.
   - ☐ **b.** carefully.
   - ☐ **c.** close to the ground.

2. Maris passed Narda after Narda
   - ☐ **a.** made a very wide turn.
   - ☐ **b.** slowed down to let Maris pass.
   - ☐ **c.** crashed into an asteroid.

3. Rel had a problem with his
   - ☐ **a.** space suit.
   - ☐ **b.** helmet.
   - ☐ **c.** engine.

4. It was not possible to land on the asteroid because it was
   - ☐ **a.** very small.
   - ☐ **b.** covered with large lakes.
   - ☐ **c.** covered with sharp mountain peaks.

5. Rel asked Maris to
   - ☐ **a.** send a rescue ship for him.
   - ☐ **b.** stay there with him.
   - ☐ **c.** help him get out of his spaceship.

6. Narda decided to
   - ☐ **a.** finish the race.
   - ☐ **b.** come back to help Rel.
   - ☐ **c.** give the medal to Maris.

7. Who won the race?
   - ☐ **a.** Maris
   - ☐ **b.** Narda
   - ☐ **c.** Melona

Vocabulary

8. Maris would lose points for communicating with Rel. The word *communicating* means
   - ☐ **a.** helping.
   - ☐ **b.** following.
   - ☐ **c.** talking.

Idioms

9. Maris had to pick up speed to pass Narda. The idiom *to pick up speed* means
   - ☐ **a.** to go faster.
   - ☐ **b.** to try harder.
   - ☐ **c.** to turn around.

10. Narda decided to hang around where the rescue ship could find her. The idiom *to hang around* means
    - ☐ **a.** to listen.
    - ☐ **b.** to stay.
    - ☐ **c.** to leave.

How many questions did you answer correctly? Circle your score. Then fill in your score on the Score Chart on page 190.

Number Correct	Score
1	10
2	20
3	30
4	40
5	50
6	60
7	70
8	80
9	90
10	100

UNDERSTANDING THE STORY

Exercise A ~ Checking Comprehension

Answer each question by writing a complete sentence. Begin each sentence with a capital letter, and end each sentence with a period. You may use the line numbers in parentheses to help you.

1. Why did Maris have to look at her charts? (7)

_____

2. What did Maris do during the next two hours? (8)

_____

3. What would happen to the ship if it got too close to the asteroid? (20)

_____

4. What did Maris see when she was halfway around the asteroid? (22)

_____

5. Why was Maris going to lose points? (31)

_____

6. Why was Rel flying slowly? (33)

_____

7. Why couldn't Rel land on the asteroid? (36)

_____

8. What did Maris tell Narda to do? (56)

_____

9. What did the rescue ship use to pull Rel's minicraft away from the asteroid? (80)

_____

10. Who won the race? (81)

_____

Exercise B ~ Building Sentences

Make sentences by adding the correct letter.

1. _____ Soon Maris was flying

2. _____ Later, she flew around

3. _____ Maris knew Rel's ship

4. _____ Rel thought he might have to

5. _____ The asteroid was

a. two small moons.

b. land on the asteroid.

c. covered with mountains.

d. swiftly through space.

e. was in trouble.

Now do questions 6–10 the same way.

6. _____ Maris thought she could

7. _____ Rel's ship was moving

8. _____ Maris was afraid they

9. _____ Later, the medal didn't seem

10. _____ You don't have to wear a medal to

a. might never be found.

b. so important.

c. still win the race.

d. be proud of yourself.

e. toward the asteroid.

Now write the sentences on the lines below. Remember to begin each sentence with a capital letter and to end each sentence with a period.

1. _____

2. _____

3. _____

4. _____

5. _____

6. _____

7. _____

8. _____

9. _____

10. _____

Exercise C ~ Adding Vocabulary

In the box are 8 words from the story. Complete each sentence by adding the correct word.

repeated	rescue	calculations	guided
gravity	perfectly	panic	instructions

1. Maris did not make a mistake. She did everything _____.

2. Narda made a very wide turn. When she _____ the turn, Maris flew past her.

3. Maris was afraid of being pulled toward the asteroid. She didn't want to

   get caught in the asteroid's _____.

4. Rel had to figure out how to stay away from the asteroid. He had to

   make the right _____.

5. Maris told Rel what to do. She gave him _____.

6. Rel was in trouble and needed help. Narda sent a ship to

   _____ him.

7. Maris was afraid that they might crash and never be found. She

   suddenly felt _____.

8. Narda showed the rescue ship where to find Rel. Narda

   _____ the ship to him.

Exercise D ~ Using Verbs Correctly

In the box are five forms of the verb *to go*. Fill in the blanks by writing the correct form of the verb. Use each word once.

go	goes	going	went	gone

1. Maris thought that she was _____ to win the Space Star medal.

2. Last week, Narda's spaceship _____ very fast.

3. Her spaceship went faster than it had ever _____ before.

4. Rel said, "I always take my helmet when I _____ out in my spaceship."

5. Every month, Narda leaves Jupiter and _____ to Earth.

Below are five forms of the verb *to fly*. Fill in the blanks by writing the correct form of the verb. Use each word once.

fly	flies	flying	flew	flown

6. Narda said, "I always _____ as fast as I can."

7. Yesterday, Rel _____ his spaceship all morning.

8. Over the years, Narda has _____ in many races.

9. When Rel is _____ his spaceship, he forgets about everything else.

10. Almost every day, Maris puts on her space suit and _____ for an hour.

Exercise E ~ Changing Statements to Questions

Change each statement to a question. Begin the question with the word or words in parentheses. Put a question mark at the end of each question.

1. Narda was flying very carefully today. (How)

   _____

2. Rel was in trouble. (Who)

   _____

3. Maris flew around two moons. (How many)

   _____

4. Rel thought that he would land on the asteroid. (Where)

   _____

5. Maris saw a spaceship in the distance. (What)

   _____

6. The rescue ship arrived a short time later. (When)

   _____

7. Maris felt happy because she helped Rel. (Why)

   _____

8. Lael J. Littke wrote "Space Star". (Who)

   _____

Exercise F ~ Vocabulary Review

Write a complete sentence for each word or group of words.

1. confidence _____

   _____

2. contestant _____

   _____

3. spectator _____

   _____

4. soar _____

   _____

5. quite a few _____

   _____

6. rescue _____

   _____

7. perfectly _____

   _____

8. communicating _____

   _____

9. pick up speed _____

   _____

10. hang around _____

   _____

STUDYING THE STORY

A. Looking Back at the Story

Discuss these questions with your partner or with the group. Your teacher may ask you to write your answer to one of the questions.

- Were you surprised that Melona, a pilot from the planet Mercury, won the race? Explain.

- If you were Maris, would you have stopped to help Rel? Why?

- Why did Narda return to Maris instead of finishing the race?

- Although Maris didn't win the race, she still felt very proud of herself. Why?

B. Using a Cluster Map to Gather Facts

In each box in the cluster map below, write on important fact about the story. Later, you will use these facts to write a *summary*. You may look back at the story.

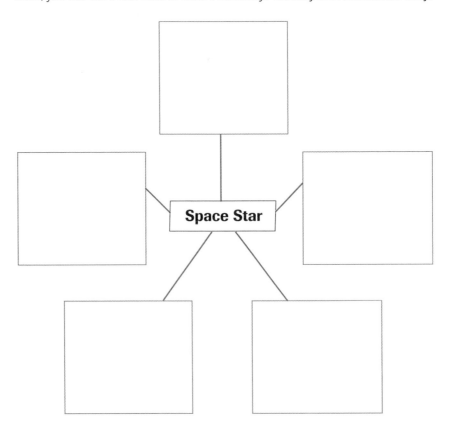

Space Star

THINKING ABOUT LITERATURE

1. A **summary** gives the main points, or facts, of a story. Use the facts in the cluster map you completed to help you write a *summary* of "Space Star."

   _____

   _____

   _____

   _____

   _____

   _____

2. "Space Star" is a **science fiction** story. Write the beginning of a *science fiction* story of your own. Use five or more of the words in the box in your story.

space	shouted	huge	landed
leader	running	believe	creature

   _____

   _____

   _____

   _____

   _____

   _____

   _____

   _____

   _____

   _____

THE CONTEST

BY WILLIAM HOFFMAN

GETTING READY TO READ

1. The Story and You

In "The Contest," you will meet Earl and his father. They are both at work, and they are working very hard. They work until they are almost too tired to move. Tell about a time when you had to work very hard. What kept you going? Did you ever start a job and then quit before you finished? Tell what happened.

2. Learning About Literature

In "The Contest," there is a **conflict** between Earl and his father. A *conflict* is a struggle or a fight. Conflict is a very important part of many stories and books. You will also find conflict in many TV shows and movies. It is exciting to discover which side or character will win.

3. Looking Ahead

Look at the picture on the left. Where are the men, and what kind of work are they doing? Think about the title of the story. What is a contest? What kind of contest might the characters be in? Read on to see if you are right.

THE CONTEST

BY WILLIAM HOFFMAN

PART 1

It was dark in the coal mine where Earl and his father were working. They turned on the light in the headlamps that they were wearing.

Earl and his father did not speak to each other. They had not spoken all day. They had not spoken since supper the evening before.

"You're not going to Detroit," Earl's father had said. "I won't let you go."

"I can get a job there," Earl had said. "Amos told me they're paying good money."

"You're not going to Detroit until I say so—and that's not until you're a man. You're not a man now! I don't want to hear anymore about it."

Earl could understand his father's anger. Earl's two older brothers had long ago left that gray, lonely country where there was only enough work to last three or four months of the year.

Earl wanted to leave his home. But he wanted his father's permission to leave. He did not want to sneak away. He wanted to go like a man. When he left, it would be by the front door.

Now, Earl and his father **made their way** through the coal mine. The headlamps shone brightly at the beginning of their shift.[1] But before their shift was over, the headlamps would have only a weak **glow**. Then Earl and his father would have to feel their way along like blind men.

They had been working together ever since Earl was sixteen. Like all of his friends, Earl had quit school as soon as the state law allowed. His father had taught him how to mine coal. The rooms in the mine were very low. They were too low for a man to stand up straight. His father had taught him how to load coal into a car while

---

1. *shift*: As used here, the word *shift* means "the hours that a person works."

lying on his side or while kneeling. Earl's father liked being a miner.
As a young man, he had set records for the number of cars he had
filled. He had always loaded more cars than anyone else. He was fifty
years old now. But he was still very strong—and proud of it.

Earl and his father got on their hands and knees. They crawled
into the room where they worked. Their picks and shovels stood
against the wall, ready to be used.

The two men began to shovel coal into the first car. They always
worked at a certain speed. As Earl's father shoveled the coal, he
suddenly changed that speed. He started to shovel the coal very
fast—much faster than ever.

At first Earl didn't realize that it was a contest. He thought that his
father was just taking out his anger on the coal. Earl had to work
very fast to keep up with his father. They quickly filled the first car.
Then they released the brake and pushed the car. The car moved
down the track.

They pulled another empty coal car into the room. They again
loaded it very quickly. Then the father shouted for more empty cars.

"Make sure we have plenty of cars!" the father told Otis Eberly,
the foreman.

Otis brought them six empty cars and took away the two cars that
were filled with coal.

When they began shoveling again, the father worked even faster
than before. He smiled. Earl knew then that his father was not angry.
He was just trying to show that he was stronger than Earl. He was
trying to prove that his son was not a man yet.

Earl began shoveling faster. He and his father rapidly filled the
next two cars. Neither of them stopped to take a drink of the water
they had brought with them. They did not stop to wipe the sweat
from their faces. They were loading the coal into the cars as fast as
they could.

Earl wished that his father would rest so that he could rest too.

But his father did not stop.

"Tired?" Earl's father asked after a while.

"I'm just getting started," Earl answered.

"Why are you sweating, then?" asked his father.

"For the same reason you are, I guess."

His father's laugh was short and hard. They both kept working at top speed. They were throwing shovel after shovel of coal into the car.

Earl's body **ached**. His elbows knocked against the hard rock floor until they began to bleed. His mouth was dry.

The two men worked on. They did not stop for lunch. Otis kept bringing more empty coal cars. Other miners came to the **entrance** of the room. They watched Earl and his father.

CHECK YOUR READING

Put an **X** in the box next to the correct answer.

Reading Comprehension

1. Where were Earl and his father working?
   - ☐ **a.** on a farm
   - ☐ **b.** in a store
   - ☐ **c.** in a coal mine

2. Earl wanted to go to
   - ☐ **a.** Detroit.
   - ☐ **b.** New York.
   - ☐ **c.** California.

3. Earl and his father had worked together ever since Earl was
   - ☐ **a.** sixteen.
   - ☐ **b.** eighteen.
   - ☐ **c.** twenty.

4. How old was Earl's father?
   - ☐ **a.** forty years old
   - ☐ **b.** fifty years old
   - ☐ **c.** sixty years old

5. Earl's father was very
   - ☐ **a.** fat.
   - ☐ **b.** weak.
   - ☐ **c.** strong.

6. On this day, Earl's father
   - ☐ **a.** worked very slowly.
   - ☐ **b.** rested often.
   - ☐ **c.** shoveled very fast.

Vocabulary

7. Earl and his father used the glow from the headlamps to see in the dark. The word *glow* means
   - ☐ **a.** light.
   - ☐ **b.** weight.
   - ☐ **c.** smell.

8. After he shoveled for many hours, Earl's body ached. The word *ached* means
   - ☐ **a.** felt good.
   - ☐ **b.** was rested.
   - ☐ **c.** hurt.

9. Miners came to the entrance of the room to watch Earl and his father. The word *entrance* means
   - ☐ **a.** floor.
   - ☐ **b.** opening.
   - ☐ **c.** walls.

Idioms

10. Earl and his father made their way through the coal mine. The idiom *made their way* means
    - ☐ **a.** lived.
    - ☐ **b.** went.
    - ☐ **c.** stopped.

How many questions did you answer correctly? Circle your score. Then fill in your score on the Score Chart on page 190.

Number Correct	Score
1	10
2	20
3	30
4	40
5	50
6	60
7	70
8	80
9	90
10	100

UNDERSTANDING THE STORY

Exercise A ~ Checking Comprehension
Answer each question by writing a complete sentence. Begin each sentence with a capital letter, and end each sentence with a period. You may use the line numbers in parentheses to help you.

1. Where were Earl and his father working? (1)

_____

2. Why did Earl want to go to Detroit? (8)

_____

3. When had Earl's two older brothers left home? (13)

_____

4. How old was Earl when he started to work with his father? (24)

_____

5. Who taught Earl how to mine coal? (26)

_____

6. How old was Earl's father? (31)

_____

7. What was Earl's father trying to prove? (53)

_____

8. Why did Earl wish that his father would rest? (60)

_____

9. What happened to Earl's elbows? (69)

_____

10. Who did the miners watch? (73)

_____

Exercise B ~ Building Sentences

Make sentences by adding the correct letter.

1. _____ At first, Earl and his father

    a. he wanted to go like a man.

2. _____ Earl wanted to leave home, but

    b. into the room where they worked.

3. _____ The rooms in the mine

    c. did not speak to each other.

4. _____ They crawled

    d. than he usually did.

5. _____ Earl's father shoveled the coal faster

    e. were very low.

Now do questions 6–10 the same way.

6. _____ Earl had to shovel very fast to

    a. as they could.

7. _____ They pushed the car

    b. keep up with his father.

8. _____ Earl knew that his father was

    c. to eat lunch.

9. _____ They worked as fast

    d. trying to beat him.

10. _____ They did not stop

    e. down the track.

Now write the sentences on the lines below. Remember to begin each sentence with a capital letter and to end each sentence with a period.

1. _____

2. _____

3. _____

4. _____

5. _____

6. _____

7. _____

8. _____

9. _____

10. _____

Exercise C ~ Adding Vocabulary

In the box are 8 words from the story. Complete each sentence by adding the correct word.

wipe	bleed	allowed	released
foreman	sneak	permission	kneeling

1. Earl wanted to leave home. However, he wanted his father's

   _____ to go.

2. Earl wanted to leave home like a man. He did not want to

   _____ away.

3. The rooms in the mine were low. They were so low that the men had to

   load coal while they were _____.

4. Earl stopped going to school as soon as he could. He left as soon as the

   state law _____.

5. Otis Eberly brought the men some empty coal cars. That was Otis's job

   because he was the _____.

6. There was sweat on his father's face. But his father did not stop to

   _____ it away.

7. Earl's elbows knocked against the hard rock floor. Soon his elbows

   began to _____.

8. Earl and his father filled the car with coal. Then they

   _____ the brake and pushed the car down the track.

Exercise D ~ Using Verbs Correctly

Fill in the blanks in each sentence to form the **past perfect tense.** Use *had* plus the **past participle** of the verb in parentheses. The first one has been done for you.

1. Earl ___*had*___ ___*left*___ school as soon as he could. (leave)

2. Earl's father _____ _____ Earl how to mine coal. (teach)

3. Ever since he was sixteen years old, Earl _____ _____ with his father. (work)

4. Amos _____ _____ Earl about a job in Detroit. (tell)

5. "You're not going to Detroit," Earl's father _____

   _____. (say)

6. As a young man, Earl's father _____ _____ many records for mining coal. (set)

7. They did not drink the water they _____ _____ with them. (bring)

8. Earl and his father _____ not _____ since the evening before. (speak)

9. Earl's father _____ _____ a miner for many years. (be)

10. Years ago Earl's brothers _____ _____ to Detroit. (go)

Write your own sentences in the **past perfect tense** by using the verbs in parentheses.

11. (had built)_____

   _____

12. (had cut) _____

   _____

Exercise E ~ True or False?

Part A

Write **T** if the sentence is true. Write **F** if the sentence is false.

1. _____ It was dark in the coal mine where Earl and his father worked.

2. _____ Earl wanted to go to California.

3. _____ Earl's father didn't want Earl to leave home.

4. _____ The rooms in the mine were very high.

5. _____ Earl's father did not like being a miner.

6. _____ Earl's father was still very strong.

7. _____ Earl's father was trying to show that Earl was not a man yet.

8. _____ Earl and his father did not eat lunch.

Part B

On the lines below, correct the three false statements.

a. _____

b. _____

c. _____

Before You Read Part 2

Earl wanted to go to Detroit. However, Earl's father said that Earl couldn't go because he wasn't a man yet. Do you think that Earl will prove he is a man? Do you think that Earl's father will let Earl go to Detroit? See if you are right.

PART 2

After a while, Earl began to lose **control** over his body. His arms began to feel weak. Coal was falling off his shovel before he lifted it over the side of the car. But his father looked as strong as ever.

"He's going to beat me," Earl thought. "He's going to beat me!
5 And if he does, he knows I won't leave home. He knows I won't go because it would look like I was running away."

So Earl kept going. "One more shovel," he said to himself over and over. "I'll do one more shovelful before I quit." The ones became tens. The tens became hundreds. The hundreds became a thousand.
10 Still his father showed no sign of **letting up**.

Then Earl saw that the **pace** was slowing. He looked at his father. Earl could see that his father was getting tired. His father was no longer smiling. His mouth was open, and he was gasping for air. He continued to lift his shovel, but each time the shovel held only a few lumps of coal.

15 Earl shoveled more slowly. He was willing to stop if his father would stop. But his father was not ready to quit.

The other miners waited at the entrance to the room. They watched without speaking.

Now Earl and his father were spilling more coal on themselves
20 than into the car. The father's face showed pain. There was fear there too. He was afraid that Earl would beat him!

Finally, the father's body would not obey him. His arms could not lift, and his fingers did not close tightly around the shovel handle. The shovel fell out of the father's hands.

25 Earl knew then that he could win! He would win if he could put *just one more shovelful* of coal into the car. He pushed his shovel into the coal. His father and the men watched. Very painfully and slowly, Earl raised the shovel.

Then Earl looked into his father's eyes. Earl saw something in his
30 father's eyes. Earl saw that his father was hoping that Earl would not shame him by **defeating** him in front of the other miners.

Earl lifted his shovel to the top of the car. He held the shovel there for a few seconds. Earl had to make sure his father understood that he was able to empty the shovel into the car. Then Earl let the

35 shovel fall to the ground.

Earl and his father fell backward. They rested their heads against the coal.

The miners began to move quietly away.

"You can go home," Otis said to the father and son. "You've
40 loaded enough coal."

Otis moved off into the darkness. Earl and his father rested on the coal. After a while Earl sat up and drank a little water. Then he passed the bottle to his father. The father poured water on his face. He got up shakily. Then they staggered out of the mine.

45 The rain had stopped. The sky was gray. Thick clouds hung in the sky. The two men could hear the sound of water from the streams.

Earl and his father did not talk until they got to the muddy road. Ahead of them was their house. It was a wooden cabin that badly needed paint. The father slowed down.

50 "You can go to Detroit," the father said. Then he asked, "Are you going to see your brothers?"

"I guess so," Earl answered.

"Tell them to write once in a while. Your mother likes to get letters."

"I'll tell them."

55 The father went into the yard. Earl followed him. His father waited for a moment at the front door. Then they entered the house together.

■

Meet the Author

William Hoffman was born in Charleston, West Virginia, in 1925. He now lives in Virginia, the state in which most of his stories take place. Hoffman's many novels and short stories are set in the South. He is known for writing plots filled with interesting characters, conflicts, and action.

CHECK YOUR READING

Put an **X** in the box next to the correct answer.

Reading Comprehension

1. After a while, Earl's arms began to feel
   - ☐ **a.** cold.
   - ☐ **b.** weak.
   - ☐ **c.** strong.

2. Earl knew his father was tired because his father
   - ☐ **a.** stopped smiling.
   - ☐ **b.** kept stopping to rest.
   - ☐ **c.** kept drinking water.

3. Earl's father was afraid that
   - ☐ **a.** Earl would beat him.
   - ☐ **b.** Earl would fight with him.
   - ☐ **c.** Earl would hurt himself.

4. Which statement is true?
   - ☐ **a.** Earl's father was glad that Earl could load so much coal.
   - ☐ **b.** None of the miners looked at Earl.
   - ☐ **c.** Earl decided not to load the last shovelful of coal.

5. Earl and his father lived in
   - ☐ **a.** a large, new house.
   - ☐ **b.** a small apartment.
   - ☐ **c.** a wooden cabin.

6. At the end of the story, Earl's father said that Earl
   - ☐ **a.** had to stay at home.
   - ☐ **b.** could go to Detroit.
   - ☐ **c.** was not yet a man.

Vocabulary

7. After Earl worked for a long time, he lost control over his body. The word *control* means
   - ☐ **a.** power.
   - ☐ **b.** weight.
   - ☐ **c.** happiness.

8. After they worked for hours, their pace got slower. The word *pace* means
   - ☐ **a.** fun.
   - ☐ **b.** speed.
   - ☐ **c.** money.

9. Earl would be defeating his father in front of the other miners. The word *defeating* means
   - ☐ **a.** helping.
   - ☐ **b.** asking.
   - ☐ **c.** winning.

Idioms

10. He kept on shoveling; he wasn't letting up. The idiom *letting up* means
    - ☐ **a.** looking sad.
    - ☐ **b.** stopping or going slower.
    - ☐ **c.** asking for food.

How many questions did you answer correctly? Circle your score. Then fill in your score on the Score Chart on page 190.

Number Correct	Score
1	10
2	20
3	30
4	40
5	50
6	60
7	70
8	80
9	90
10	100

UNDERSTANDING THE STORY

Exercise A ~ Checking Comprehension

Answer each question by writing a complete sentence. Begin each sentence with a capital letter, and end each sentence with a period. You may use the line numbers in parentheses to help you.

1. How did Earl's arms feel after a while? (1)

_____

2. Why wouldn't Earl leave home if his father beat him shoveling coal? (5)

_____

3. What was Earl's father afraid of? (21)

_____

4. What fell out of the father's hands? (24)

_____

5. What did Earl have to do to win? (25)

_____

6. What was Earl's father hoping? (30)

_____

7. What did the father pour on his face? (43)

_____

8. What did the two men hear? (46)

_____

9. When did Earl and his father talk? (47)

_____

10. What did their house look like? (48)

_____

Exercise B ~ Building Sentences

Make sentences by adding the correct letter.

1. _____ Earl felt weak, but his father   **a.** his father would stop.

2. _____ Earl was willing to stop if   **b.** beaten before.

3. _____ Finally, the shovel fell out   **c.** still looked strong.

4. _____ Then Earl looked into   **d.** of his father's hands.

5. _____ Earl's father had never been   **e.** his father's eyes.

Now do questions 6–10 the same way.

6. _____ Earl lifted his shovel   **a.** the house together.

7. _____ The father poured water   **b.** the bottle to his father.

8. _____ Earl drank some water and then gave   **c.** on his face.

9. _____ They did not talk until   **d.** to the top of the car.

10. _____ The father and son went into   **e.** they got to the road.

Now write the sentences on the lines below. Remember to begin each sentence with a capital letter and to end each sentence with a period.

1. _____

2. _____

3. _____

4. _____

5. _____

6. _____

7. _____

8. _____

9. _____

10. _____

Exercise C ~ Adding Vocabulary

In the box are 8 words from the story. Complete each sentence by adding the correct word.

muddy	streams	darkness	spilling
gasping	staggered	lumps	shame

1. The shovel was nearly empty. It held just a few _____ of coal.

2. Earl's father was getting tired. His mouth was open and he was

   _____ for air.

3. Earl and his father had trouble lifting their shovels to the edge of the car.

   They kept _____ coal on themselves.

4. Earl's father was worried. He was afraid that Earl would

   _____ him in front of the other men.

5. Otis turned away from the light. Then he moved off into the

   _____.

6. Earl and his father had trouble walking. They _____ as they left the mine.

7. They heard the sound of water. The water came from nearby

   _____.

8. The men went to the cabin. They walked along a _____ road.

Exercise D ~ Using Verbs Correctly

Fill in each blank by writing **present, past,** or **future** to show the tense of the verb in each sentence. The first one has been done for you.

1. In a few months, Earl will leave home. _____ *future* _____

2. Earl pushed his shovel into the coal. _____

3. The shovel fell out of the father's hands. _____

4. The miners stare at Earl and his father. _____

5. Earl drinks some water from the bottle. _____

6. The father went into the house. _____

7. Earl will write letters to his mother and father. _____

8. Earl's mother likes to get letters. _____

9. His father waited at the front door. _____

10. Earl's mother and father will visit him in Detroit. _____

Fill in each blank by writing **present perfect, past perfect,** or **past continuous** to show the tense of the verb in each sentence. The first one has been done for you.

11. Coal was falling off the shovel. _____ *past continuous* _____

12. Earl and his father were spilling coal on themselves. _____

13. Earl's father had done his best. _____

14. The rain has stopped. _____

15. Earl has been a miner for a few years. _____

16. Earl's father had been a miner for most of his life. _____

17. He had worked in the mines for nearly thirty years. _____

18. The miners were watching Earl and his father. _____

Exercise E ~ Combining Sentences

Combine the two sentences into one. Write the new sentence on the line.

1. Earl's arms felt tired. They felt weak.

_____

2. The father's face showed pain. It also showed fear.

_____

3. Earl felt very tired. His father felt very tired too.

_____

4. Otis spoke to Earl's father. He also spoke to Earl.

_____

5. Earl sat up. He drank a little water.

_____

6. Thick clouds hung in the sky. The sky was gray.

_____

7. Their house was a wooden cabin. It was old.

_____

8. Earl's father entered the house. Earl entered the house with him.

_____

Exercise F ~ Vocabulary Review

Write a complete sentence for each word or group of words.

1. permission _____

_____

2. bleed _____

_____

3. allowed _____

_____

4. entrance _____

_____

5. made their way _____

_____

6. darkness _____

_____

7. gasping _____

_____

8. staggered _____

_____

9. control _____

_____

10. letting up _____

_____

STUDYING THE STORY

A. Looking Back at the Story

Discuss these questions with your partner or with the group. Your teacher may ask you to write your answer to one of the questions.

- Why do you think Earl wanted to go to Detroit? Why do you think Earl's father wanted Earl to stay home?

- Earl could have put the final shovelful of coal into the car, but he decided to let the shovel fall to the ground. Why did Earl do that?

- Why did Earl's father finally agree to let Earl go to Detroit?

- Suppose that Earl's father said that Earl still couldn't go to Detroit. What do you think Earl would have done?

B. Using a Graphic Organizer to Compare and Contrast Characters

Use the graphic organizer below to **compare and contrast** Earl with his father. In the boxes, list how the two men are *alike* and how they are *different*.

Earl and His Father

How are they alike?	How are they different?

THINKING ABOUT LITERATURE

1. The **motive** is the reason behind a character's actions. It is *why* a character acts the way he or she does. On the lines below, explain the father's *motive* for starting a contest with Earl.

_____

_____

_____

_____

_____

2. Here is your chance to be a character in a story. Suppose that you are Earl and that you have moved to Detroit. After two weeks, you decide to write a letter to your father. In your letter, tell what has happened to you since you left home. Did you get a job? Do you have some new friends? Where are you living? Use your imagination when you write the letter.

_____
Date

Dear Dad,

_____

_____

_____

_____

_____

_____

_____

_____

_____

_____

Love,
Earl

IRREGULAR VERBS

Present Tense	Past Tense	Past Participle
be (am/is/are)	was/were	began
become	became	become
begin	began	begun
build	built	built
buy	bought	bought
catch	caught	caught
cut	cut	cut
come	came	come
die	died	died
do	did	done
draw	drew	drawn
drive	drove	driven
eat	ate	eaten
fall	fell	fallen
find	found	found
fly	flew	flown
get	got	gotten
give	gave	given
go	went	gone
grow	grew	grown
have	had	had
hear	heard	heard
hold	held	held
keep	kept	kept
know	knew	known
leave	left	left
lie	lay	lain
lose	lost	lost
make	made	made
put	put	put
ride	rode	ridden
run	ran	run
say	said	said
see	saw	seen
sell	sold	sold
send	sent	sent

Present Tense	Past Tense	Past Participle
set	set	set
shake	shook	shaken
sing	sang	sung
sit	sat	sat
sleep	slept	slept
speak	spoke	spoken
spend	spent	spent
steal	stole	stolen
strike	struck	struck
take	took	taken
teach	taught	taught
tell	told	told
think	thought	thought
throw	threw	thrown

SCORE CHART

This is the Score Chart for **CHECK YOUR READING**. Shade in your score for each part of the story. For example, if your score was 80 for Part 1 of **Something Funny**, look at the bottom of the chart for Part 1, **Something Funny**. Shade in the bar up to the 80 mark. By looking at this chart, you can see how well you did on each part of the story.

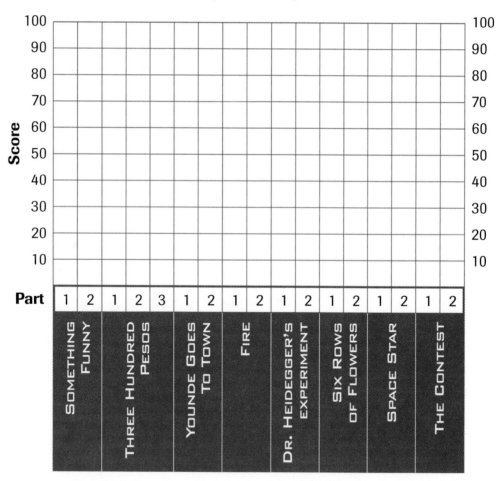